The Four Aces

This is the best yet! I just finished it. This is so exciting. I loved the descriptions of the weddings. The minute it arrived, I started reading, and I couldn't put it down until I finished it.

—Donna B., RN, CA

A good story to wind the day down with, while savoring words, humor, likeable and not- such-likeable characters, with small town flavor and thickening plots filled with secrets while deep connections unfold.

—Sharon N., OR

Wow! I found myself stealing time from other activities to read because I wanted to know what happened next. What a curious and intriguing read."

—Kelly E. A., Austin, TX

The Children's Home Mystery Series 1-6
by Marilyn R. Stark

The Flutist and the Dancer
This is a story of a six-year-old girl who is left at the Children's Home by her grandmother. She arrives with a rag doll and an unusual nursery-rhyme book. Her grandmother gives the administration a false name and never returns. The trauma of being taken from her loving Nanny and her twin brother results in a memory block against which she struggles all the way through adolescence.

The Pianist and the Locksmith
This novel steps back to World War II and is about the lengths SaraBeth, a young mother, will go to when it comes to protecting her children and the inner battle she has with her abusive father. This is about faith, trust, and forgiveness between SaraBeth, her high-school sweetheart who spent years in a military hospital and their families.

Broken Arrows, Broken Promises
A bachelor minister's prayers battle with the revelation of his secret past. His first love, Tessa, has a daughter, and she too is searching for information. She hires private detective Will Fox, who is torn between helping her and finding his mother's Native American "story arrows."

Trails End Isle & Wings
Jonothan loves to fly, but he can't fly from his father's deathbed request. If only a 1931 Ford Pickup Truck could talk. In the search he also meets his dad's two other children, Jace and Samantha, and sparks fly.

Brandi also seems bent on learning her lessons in life the hard way. After working with the Shadow Angels and her

Reader Reviews for Marilyn R. Stark's Books

The Flutist and the Dancer

I feel the writing is best when it renders the inner life of the main character and the wonderful way she has of experiencing the world around her. The reader comes away with a clear and moving experience of what it must be like for children in foster home situations. The novel definitely has a universal appeal.
—Dr. Richard Messer, Bowling Green State University

Real emotional. It takes you there with its continual turns and surprises. This most descriptive book took me on a journey back 56 years – through each door, up each step, into each room of vivid wonderful and painful memories.
—Donna B., RN

I liked the seed of mystery from beginning to end. It kept me guessing and interested. Marilyn has a unique candor as she reveals the characters and allows the reader to feel akin to Shannon's soul.
—Grace G., Secretary of the Lima Area Writers Club

I've enjoyed reading this book and find the similes and metaphors effective—they provoke smiles and nods from time to time—very apt. The writing style is smooth.
—Catherine Bauer, Creative Writing Teacher and Author

I didn't want to put it down. I loved your book. It gives you a warm feeling – inside. It's what we call a sit-by-the-fireside and read book. Very descriptive. The way you make the reader feel. How do I know a book is good? If it makes you laugh, or cry, or feel—it's good.
—Alice, Library Public Relations Representative

The Pianist and the Locksmith

The author dramatizes a truth that we often overlook in our hectic, fragmented lives today: That the problems that originate in family life can only be solved through family interaction, love, and good will. The deepest truths of our lives are secrets.

—Dr. Richard Messer, Bowling Green State University

Broken Arrows/Broken Promises

I kept wanting to come back for more until I had finished the final page. That's the mark of a good book It has light romance, adventure and mystery. I'm comfortable recommending Marilyn's books to a broad range of people from teens to senior adults.

—Kathy S., Bookmobile, Lima, OH

What a story! The third in her series. Her best writing so far. Intriguing, inspirational, and filled with numerous twists, turns and surprises. The author put me there at the wedding – and I felt I could close my eyes and walk through her early Victorian Era house. Adapted for TV would be Lifetime Hallmark movies for the entire family to enjoy. The three books would make a good series. A True Fan of Marilyn's writings.

Gwendolyn, Crossville, TN

Safe Passage in Masquerade

Stark presents lovable, memorable characters in another interesting twisted plot readers have come to expect in her Children's Home Mystery Series. Just when you think you have almost figured out the answers to all the questions, she tosses in a tidbit that makes you realize she's tricked you. Now you'll have to read clear to the end...and it's always worth the wait!

—Pat Rodabaugh

Children's Home sister, Shannon, she becomes a Deputy Sheriff. And she has to learn how to trust from an unlikely teacher: a German Shepherd pup named Pepper.

Safe Passage in Masquerade

Mason Davies, Interim Caretaker of the Marblehead Lighthouse on Lake Erie, rescues a young woman from a disabled vehicle during a snow storm. As an adoptee from the children's home, he knows what it is like to need someone, but she has trouble trusting anyone.

Jonothan returns to Turtle Crossing to start his career with Miss Bea in her real estate business. The Shadow Angels recruit him to keep Bea safe. But from whom?

Prior to a wedding ceremony at the Welby Falls, Rev. C.W. announced, "Following the ceremony, don't miss the history and future of the Tunnels and Turtle Crossing."

The Four Aces

Shannon and David's twin daughters return to Turtle Crossing after acquiring their dream professions—Lily as a chiropractor and Lori as a veterinarian. Their brother Hunter and cousin Storm have orders to protect the twins. While dealing with a break-in, their trained instincts lead them to becoming The Four Aces.

During the family reunion at Granny's Estate, they discover two toddlers that have been mysteriously abandoned and immediately must protect these children from the hands of a former classmate who, if he had his way, would turn the children over to child protective services immediately despite the danger doing so would bring.

The newly formed Aces move to protect these children from being lost to true family forever, like their Mom, Shannon had.

Published by Workplay Publishing
Newton, KS 67114

workplaypublishing.com

Copyright © 2022 Marilyn R. Stark. All rights reserved.

Cover design and interior layout by André Swartley. Photos used with permission.

ISBN 978-1-7343946-4-1

PRINTED IN THE UNITED STATES OF AMERICA

How Writing

CHANGED MY LIFE

a memoir in prose and poetry

MARILYN R. STARK

Workplay Publishing

Contents

BLUE

Life stories (Mar 2021)	18
The Child in Me (Sep 2017)	19
Forsythia's Surprise (May 1982)	20
My dad's family dinners (Jun 2021)	22
Hens, Roosters and Baby Chicks (Jan 2018)	25
Back to the Country (Jun 2021)	27
Pastime Park (Aug 2021)	30
The Changing of the Seasons (Nov 2015)	41
The Borrowed Christmas Tree (Dec 2002)	44
I Surprised Myself (Aug 2021)	46
A Full Moon Reflected (Aug 2021)	49
The Velveteen Steel River (Apr 2021)	52
Keys (Aug 2017)	54
Children's Home Wake Up and Wiggle Bell (Dec 1989)	55
A Summer Morning (Jul 1976)	59
My First Pair of High Heels (Jan 2022)	60
Lavender Blossoms (Nov 1982)	64
First Kiss (May 2015)	65
Lavender—Rose & Marigold Lace (Apr 2017)	70
New Clothes and White Sweater (Jun 2021)	71
Christmas News 2004 (Dec 2004)	74
The Study Room (Aug 1952)	75
A Novel Story and Muse (Apr 2018)	78
A Collection of Memories (Dec 1994)	79
Choices. Goals. Dreams. (Jan 2022)	80

A Master Plan (Jan 2010)	85
Sometimes Everyone Needs Someone (Nov 2021)	87
Alone? (1979)	90
My Wedding Dress in Powder Blue (Oct 2020)	91
Recipe for Happiness (Nov 2001)	94
The Pocket Mouse (Mar 1981)	95
Our First Trip to Virginia (Jan 2022)	96
The Dance (Jan 2018)	98
A Moment in Time (Jan 2021)	101
When I First Arrived in Lima (Aug 2021)	103
Time Marches On (May 2014)	106
Don was Bowling (Sep 2021)	108
Full-Time Mom (Nov 2016)	110
Fences and Gossip (Jan 2022)	112
Smile and Pass it On (May 2012)	116
Pigeon Lake Storm (Jun 2021)	117
The Swamp (Jun 1982)	120
The Neighborhood Party Line (Apr 2013)	121
Release…The Butterfly (Dec 1994)	125
Life Isn't Always a Matter of Choice (Apr 2020)	126
Marking Time (Jul 1990)	128
The Soul and the Spirit (May 2018)	129
Before Writing *The Flutist and the Dancer* (Oct 2021)	131
The Patchwork Quilt (Aug 1984)	134
Children's Home Reunion Derailed (Jul 2021)	135
The Reunion (Nov 1987)	140
Finding My Way in the Field of Writing (Aug 2021)	142
Family History Mystery (Sep 1991)	144
July 30, 1951: Forever Destined (Jun 1991)	146
Writing Challenges (Aug 2021)	149
Visit a Touch of the Past Today (n.d.)	154
Rain in New Orleans (Apr 2010)	156

Timeless, Dignified, Always in Style (May 2009)	157
Atlantic Beach (May 2009)	159
While Observing Two People at the Grocery (Jan 2018)	161
I Am You (Jul 1979)	164
Bell's Palsy (Oct 2017)	166
Unexpected Winner (Apr 2009)	169

GRAY

Memories Clarified (May 2022)	172
A Letter to My Mom (Nov 2018)	173
A Pickled Patience Personified Promise (Sep 2016)	186
Photographs (1980)	190
Sister, Differences and Connections (Apr 2021)	191
Two Little Girls (Nov 1980)	197
A Step Father (Feb 1981)	198
George was Creative (Oct 2009)	199
Grieving and Thanskgiving (Oct 2009)	201
Susie, Until We Meet Again... (Oct 2009)	203
Susie (Aug 2020)	204
Going Home (Sep 2014)	206
Enduring the Loss of a Child (n.d.)	214
Sisters Visit (Sep 1984)	217
Dolls in Crochet, Leather and Lace (Nov 2021)	219
I Heard the Bells on Christmas Day (Dec 2021)	220
My Rainbow (Dec 1981)	221
Promised Snow but I Stole Off to Paradise (Mar 2015)	222
Life is a Timeless Momentous Journey (n.d.)	224
Our World had Stopped (Nov 2014)	225
Dearly Beloved (Nov 2014)	228
It was Monday Evening (Dec 2014)	230
Dreams & Dancing (Dec 2015)	233
How are You Doing? (Dec 2014)	234

The Ohio Travels of Daniel and Alice (n.d.)	236
My First Bus Tour—The Summer Before 9/11 (n.d.)	239
Midnight (Dec 2015)	241
Live Your LIfe (Nov 2014)	243
My Former Destination (2015)	245
For the Last Time (Jan 2015)	246
Just One More Time (Dec 2001)	248
I'm Doing Okay (Feb 2015)	250
Life's Ever Changing Challenges (Feb 2018)	252
Milestone Options (Jun 2015)	253
Together or Apart (Apr 2015)	255
Sunday Morning (Oct 1990)	257
Time Rides the White Stallion (Nov 1985)	258
From Her Favorite Rocking Chair (Oct 1991)	260
A White Haze (Sep 1991)	262
The Hitchhiker (Jan 2022)	264
Randy's Funeral (Aug 2018)	269
We've Named a Star Randy (Jul 2018)	272
Superior Coach (Apr 2022)	273
Born on Labor Day (Apr 2022)	276
The Day Christal was Born (May 2022)	279
Sean was Born in the Spring (May 2022)	282
Don's Sisters (Mar 2022)	285
Acceptance? Never! (Mar 1986)	288
The Celebration of Russel G's Life (May 2018)	290
Remembering Nola (Mar 2016)	293
Harold's Legacy (Feb 2009)	296
Remembering Nadine (Feb 2022)	298
Song of Farewell (Jul 1980)	300
Unexpected Adieu (Apr 1992)	302
A Visit with my Aunt Lou (Jun 1999)	303
Aunt Marjorie, Goodbye at Ninety-Eight (Nov 2021)	305

WHITE

Words in Motion (Dec 2002)	308
Boulevard (Jan 2021)	310
Family Christmas Celebration (Jan 1991)	311
Fourth of July Conversation (Jul 1981)	313
A Handkerchief? (1988)	316
A Lady Revealed (Dec 1988)	317
A Million Years Ago? I Wonder... (1981)	319
White Elephant (Dec 1990)	321
An Artist's Palette of Ohio's Fall (Oct 1991)	322
Artificial Intelligence (Oct 2018)	324
Beginning Again (Aug 2015)	326
Cherished Memories Collections (Aug 2021)	327
Cooling Thoughts to Mow By (1996)	328
Dear Erika (Jul 1980)	329
Detroit's Auto Jewels (2008)	330
Disney World—Epcot—MGM (May 1991)	331
Ecstasy (Nov 1981)	333
Erica, A Second Birthday (Nov 1981)	334
Fractured Time of the Caregiver (Mar 2013)	335
Honeysuckle Wine (1990)	337
Grandmas (n.d.)	338
Haikus (Apr 2011)	339
Home After Surgery (Dec 1987)	340
In Answer to a Prayer (Dec 1999)	342
It's About Time (Jan 2016)	344
Let Me Tell You a Story (Dec 2003)	345
Mended? (Feb 2022)	347
My Shadow and Me (Oct 2016)	348
My Two Grandmas (May 1980)	349
New Beginnings (2015)	351

Ohio's October Masquerade (Nov 1991)	353
One Last Visit—One Last Goodbye (May 1999)	355
Our Annual Family Christmas (Dec 1992)	356
Our Thank You Love Anniversary Cake (Feb 1989)	358
Replaced (Nov 2017)	359
Research (Sep 2015)	360
September into October (Oct 2010)	361
Snowy Sweet-Scene Dream (n.d.)	363
"Slick—Sleet—Snow"	364
Polar Vortex (Jan 2014)	366
Spring & March Fog (Mar 2020)	368
Stars to Hitch a Ride On (Jul 1989)	369
Tasha, the Orphaned Lamb (May 2016)	370
The ABCs of My Roman Rooms (Apr 2017)	372
Cocoon (Nov 1981)	374
Tri-Storied Barn (Dec 1987)	375
The Traveling Knight (Aug 2000)	377
Turn of the Century (May 2012)	379
Why People Downsize (Aug 2015)	380
Willie Nelson Performs Free Concert (Dec 2000)	381
You Needed a Makeover (Apr 2017)	383
If Today Were My Last" (Mar 1981)	384
Author's Note	385
Acknowledgements	389
About the Author	391

My Memoir is dedicated to:
   My fans, family, friends old and new.

May my writing
result in a smile, plus a nod of your
      head now and then. But have
         you had your world turned
            upside-down a time or two,

questioned others' decisions,
      sometimes your own?
         Try keeping a daily journal.
            Believe. Have Faith the Lord
               really does hear our prayers.

May your heart find
   understanding
      and continued
         peaceful moments.

BLUE

My life stories are
set in pockets of time.

Some of them overlap
in bits and pieces like
a puzzle, captured from
my memory.

A page of poetry
momentarily fills in the
space-in-time, in-
between the stories.

Followed by chapters about
family and friends, writing
challenges, letter to my Mom,
and the rest of the story
in poetry.

"The Child In Me"

The child in me
  is still so naïve!
for more has
  always been

expected of me.
  Whether I'm
quiet or chatty
  it seems

there's always
  something I
need to change.
  Try and do

my very best,
  to read, listen,
and believe.
By trusting the

Lord, my head
  bowed in prayer.
Perhaps this
  heart must

just strive to
  preserve my
right to write
  and be me.

"Forsythia's Surprise"

Forsythia in full bloom. It's
   blossoms are like a spotlight
of bright sunshine
   on a cloudy day—

Greeting Daylight Savings
   Time while lawns spurt
spring growth, and fields
   are fitted to sifting brown.

Rhubarb's deep green leaves
   top red stems promising
more than one mouth-
   watering delight.

A deep-throated bird
   sounds like a cross between a frog and a hen
   that just laid a square
egg, keeps croaking in my
   tall Ewe shrubs.

Fall-pruned Forsythia branches
   became one more layer on the
compost pile. Would burial be
   their demise? Come April, I

unearthed Mother Nature's
   surprise. Composted branch-

lings revealed tiny yellow
   blossoms tipped with fragile
new roots, soon planted in the sun.

Thus, writing awakens thoughts,
   and buried memories from the
subconscious sphere—remembered
   childhood happenings, thorns,
     blessings and tears.

Marilyn with her mom & dad

My dad's family dinners weren't anything special or different than most. There was always a field where they played soft ball when the weather was nice. We usually had fried chicken (mainly because Grandma butchered her own), mashed potatoes, gravy, veggies and pies in the summer of 1941.

Once in a while they moved the heavy-duty oak kitchen table to make room for square dancing. Three of my aunts played guitar and Dad may have done some of the calling, because I had watched and heard him call at a dance hall.

At one of these Sunday dinners, we were all seated, and I have no idea what I did or said after I made a face when I tasted one of Uncle Ivan's olives. (I still never acquired a taste for olives.) I apparently talked back to Mom, and she expected me to respect her when she remarked, "If I was any closer I would…"

I must have been showing off, or perhaps testing just how far I could go, when I sassed, "You can't reach me."

Mom may have only been 4'10" tall—but she reached across that table and knocked me off my book/booster chair. I would have hit the floor, but thanks to Uncle Ivan, he stuck his knee out and broke my fall. I was in the first grade. I knew better.

I apparently didn't learn my lesson though because we were still living in the house near Collins where Carol was born when Mom told me to do something or she was going to warm my britches.

My cocky reply was, "You can't catch me," and I took off running and crawled under a bed to hide. Sure enough, she used the broom to sweep me out of hiding and by the time I scampered out, she had built up enough steam that ended in a few spanks on my behind, and a dandy talking to.

Something happened to me that day. Dad must have been out of town longer than usual again. Later, I heard her crying alone in her bedroom, while we were supposed to have been playing outside. Weeks later, we moved to the city where I finished the first grade.

I usually wore the sister/mom hat because my sisters were my responsibility. I can't recall a tree in sight, and the house was close to the sidewalk and the street. This one day, we found a bit of shade by sitting on the running board of the car parked near the house. Then, Susie got tired of riding in my little red wagon with our baby sister, and decided to help push while I already had one knee in the wagon and pushed with my other leg.

The next thing I knew, she crumbled onto the sidewalk. I thought she had died and ran in the house, carrying six month old Carol in my arms. Susie survived. She was dehydrated, and apparently came close to having heat stroke.

We were living in this house when Mom took Susie with her shopping and I stayed with Carol. She dirtied her diaper and I couldn't figure out how to clean her bottom, so I lifted her into a tri-cornered sink. Since she barely fit, there was no chance she would drown. Then, Mom and Susie arrived.

One of Mom's brothers came to live with us for a few

weeks when we lived here. He rolled his own cigarettes, and Susie, always being helpful, fed my prize goldfish with tobacco. That ended my goldfish.

"Hens, Roosters and Baby Chicks"

The sound of a rooster
  or two, crowing at sunrise.

A brooder house
  filled with five
dozen golden feathered
  baby chicks peeping
and wetting the urine-
  soaked bed of straw.

That summer it was my
  job to shovel out the
rank, breath-stealing mess
  and replace it with dry,
sweet-smelling straw.

The cluck, cluck, cluck of
  the hens as they
rhythmically bobbed their
  heads, and pecked-up
handfuls of grain tossed
  their way in the chicken yard.

And I learned how to
  gently—but quickly slip
my hand under the Queen-
  Layers and steal their eggs
for our breakfast.

But, once in awhile, an
   independent, rogue hen
would slip out of the gate,
   find a nesting place, and
later come out of hiding,
   proudly herding her very
own six to ten peeping baby
   chicks.

Counting, as she swept
   them into the shade of an
ancient cottonwood tree,
   she stretched and fluttered
her massive wings to shelter
   her babies. Then, finally tucking
her head under her wing,
   their peeping stopped.

From a distance, she appeared
   to be a fat, round, uninteresting
basket of cotton to the predator
   circling overhead.

Marilyn, age 4

Marilyn, age 3, with her dad

Usually, Dad found another place for his family to live whenever he felt like it or was driving for another company, but during this time period, in 1942, I would have been in the second grade. A family member had a group-photo taken near Green Springs. Besides, a couple of cousins recalled visiting us at this farm in the country.

I loved this farm. You won't see a mother duck teaching her little ones as they follow her on a cool summer afternoon in a rippling brook—in the city.

This was also a place where Dad already had plans on how he could make some extra money. He bought two turkeys to fatten-up for Thanksgiving. Keep one and sell the other. However, he found that turkeys like to fly—to a degree that he had to clip their wings, just to keep them corralled in the barn.

He purchased a piglet to raise for the same reason. However because it kept rooting under the fence he had built, he knew there was only one way he could put a stop to that. I can still see him chasing that pig to put a ring in its nose. But I hid so he wouldn't see me giggling at how many times he wiped out. He had as much mud on him as the pig.

But he finally caught that squealing little rascal—got him into a choke-hold, just as his neighbor stopped by. Between the two of them, they got the pig to calm down by grabbing his ears and pierced that ring into the pig's nose. I've been told, you know pigs smell, well so does an outhouse. But the momma skunk and her babies Dad hit one foggy night takes first place. It can steal your breath away.

He also set traps that first winter. He stretched and tacked the skins of muskrat, raccoon, and mink onto boards which were hung on the building side of the screened-in back porch. These hides paid well in those days. This meant checking those traps every day.

The first night we spent in this house, the three of us girls slept on the kitchen floor because there wasn't time to set up our beds. Moving should have been a breeze by now, plus the cleaning.

I heard a scratching sound, opened my eyes and there was a well-fed rat. I didn't know I could scream. Not only did I frighten that rat, but woke Mom and Dad. "I saw it go under the refrigerator." Dad gave me a hammer and told me to hit it with the hammer if it came out again. I doubt we slept there the following night because they probably wouldn't appreciate being awakened two nights in a row.

Odd that this is one of the few Christmases I remember having such a lovely tree. Perhaps it is because it was also the first time I was awakened hearing their voices in anger. Whatever I heard made my heart sad.

In later years, if and when I figured things out, it appeared that whenever Dad and Mom were working together in an atmosphere that meant financially they were on the same page, the same someone who had chased him for years—quite possibly found a way to intervene in their marriage once again, or perhaps this was a lifestyle he hadn't really changed after all.

Susie & Marilyn holding Carol

Pastime Park was located north of Tiffin, in Seneca County, Ohio on State Route 53, about half-way between Tiffin and Fremont, just a few miles outside of Old Fort.

The summer of 1943 before I started the third grade, Dad had once again moved us closer to the company that had just hired him. But also moved us from a sprawling farm house into an upstairs apartment in Old Fort. We had become accustomed to the country. There had been a chance to plant flowers and a garden. I thought Dad had loved it as well as Mom.

I had heard stories about the trains that ran through Continental. Mom must have thought she was dreaming of the home where she had grown-up, when she recognized the unmistakable sound of a train—passing a crossing.

She opened the door that exited from our living room onto the screened-in patio she was standing on, that doubled as a shelter for the street below. Once the train rumbled through, she unfolded a chair and stopped when she over-heard two men talking below.

"I thought you were through with renters after that last group."

"Yes. Too noisy for me."

"What do you know about this family?"

"Well, he's one of Gilmore's new drivers, with a clean record and well experienced driving just about any type of rig."

"The new renter's wife asked my wife if she knew of

anyone hiring part-time, when she stopped in at the post office to mail a letter. She said she was sending her new address to her mom, and was checking to see if there were any jobs available."

Mom didn't find any jobs listed on the cork board at the post office, but got excited about a notice that was offering the chance to seal goodies in a tin to send to the military. She collected some of the cookies she had baked the day before, wrote a letter, including a picture of her daughters, a few candy bars, cigarettes, gum and a small bag of pretzels if there was room to fill a half-gallon tin that would be sealed and mailed to her brother.

When I asked, "Where are we going?" Mom replied, "We're going to the Cannery. It is located behind the Old Fort School. A poster in the post office suggested we can send goodies to your uncle who is serving in the Army in the Pacific." I introduced Mom to the parent of a girl who said we would be in the third grade together.

Mom hadn't had the chance to make friends with anyone but family for years. After a few extra deep breaths, to gather the courage to find another place for us—on her own for a change, she had started talking to the lady she had met at the post office.

"We have just moved from a huge farm house into an upstairs apartment. My daughters and I need a place to explore. Do you know of any place that is empty or for rent?"

"How good is your imagination?" That same afternoon—her new friend drove us to Pastime Park.

During my parents nine years of marriage, I had overheard more than one person ask Mom where her husband was—and except Sunday dinners at his mom's, he was usually tied-up with his rig in another state.

However this was the first time she had had so much time on her hands and started noticing how many of the other drivers were home with their families for evening meals. Some of this information came about when my friends talked about their dads.

Mom never mentioned being upset but I had overheard more than one heated conversation between her and Dad.

She quickly found out how fast gossip traveled through this group of men. All of a sudden,

Dad showed up and suggested, "I have a big surprise for you. I think you'll be pleased."

It was apparent that Pastime Park, a Road Side Rest Area, had been ignored for some time. When Dad opened the back door of the house—he barely looked inside, but quickly closed it due to the buzzing of a swarm of bees that had had prior residence for some time.

This two-story Caretaker's House had a nice front porch as well as its private privy (outhouse) behind the house. A half-acre grassy area that needed mowing, and a picnic table near the stoned parking area for travelers' use would need to be replaced.

It was the summer of 1943. Our family appeared to be at its best during these years at Pastime Park. My parents were working together as a team, and appeared to be excited about yet another move. Surely there wouldn't be time for Dad to see other women now. Right?

This road-side rest also included a building that offered possibilities. A carport attached to the west side of this building sheltered a gas pump—which offered easy access to the one-quarter acre stone parking area along State Route 53.

The stone path to the two double-hole privies for the public—one for LADIES and the other marked MEN was in need of a coat or two of paint—plus new wiring for lights—for the evening traveler. One of her responsibilities would be to keep these privies clean, but also keep fresh toilet paper and make certain the lights were working.

One year, during Halloween, Dad stayed up all night with his shotgun loaded with buckshot to make certain no one attempted to tip over the out-houses (which was easy because they have no foundations).

The Possibilities Building became The Park Restaurant. But first, the roof needed a coat of tar. We were told to stay away from that area because Dad didn't want to worry about us getting hurt. However telling Susie to stay in the house was a waste of time. She slipped out of the house and was too close to the building when Dad tossed an empty bucket to the ground.

She yelled when the bucket landed—and got a few sprinkles of tar in her hair. Mom tried to wash it out, but ended up quickly cutting her hair that was stuck to this black sticky tar—in odd places. My first thought was—if Susie looked in a mirror, and she could get her hands on the scissors…

Mom told me a dozen times that she tied me to the clothes line when she was busy out-doors because I was always in with the chickens.

I don't recall if she didn't do that with Susie after the

tar deal. However, Mom was planning to put a new light bulb in this wall lamp, and had removed the old light bulb, climbed down the ladder to get rid of it and replace it with a new one.

Just that fast, Susie started up the ladder. I knew enough not to tell her to get down, but it wouldn't have mattered. She may have only been four years old, but she was curious and speedy. She was peeking inside the empty socket when Mom yelled, but it was too late. Susie stuck her finger in the empty space and got knocked off that ladder onto a couch nearby.

She didn't break anything that I recall or she would have been at the doctor's office.

Cleaning the interior of the restaurant kept my parents very busy. One day there was this huge empty space, and then somewhere they found two glass display cases, a cash register, curtains for the windows, a few round tables plus a few chairs. Whatever was needed in the kitchen surely included an iron skillet, grill, tea kettle, and coffee pot.

One day, I arrived home from school and was proud of what had been done to the oak plank floor. I sat down on one of the chairs. The sun left a beam across the glossy dust-free dining room floor.

There were three doors into the restaurant. One on the west side entrance from the gas pump, so Mom had easy access to and from the gas pump, one out the back from the kitchen and one on the north side that faced the house and entrance for patrons.

Mom was expected to offer full service at the gas pump, which meant: Check the oil, check the level in the battery, check the water level in the radiator or overflow, wash the windows, and of course, pump the gas.

One morning, someone appeared at the back door of our house. He wasn't asking for a handout, but offered to mow the grassy area between our house, the restaurant, the traveler's privies, to the edge of the stoned parking area. His clothes were worn and dusty, but it appeared that he had stopped at the pump and washed his face, hands and hair which were still wet. The pump was between the picnic table area and the front of our house.

After Mom showed him where the mower and gas was located, she explained, "Your Dad said, he wouldn't be surprised to see a hobo show-up because we are so close to the Nickle Plate that ran east and west through Old Fort, but to notify his boss to see if someone could stop by if he was on the road." But instead, she had several friends who she wouldn't hesitate to call.

This was during World War II. Peanuts were scarce, so roasted soy beans were used in place of peanuts in candy bars such as Hershey Bars and Bun.

It didn't take long before students would arrive to buy pop, a candy bar, chips or gum, and loved handing me their money, just to watch this eight-year-old make change back to them.

Mom had found a children's table and chairs, plus a play pen for my sisters in a space behind the display cases, yet not out of Mom's sight when she was in the kitchen. Susie was four now and had taken on wearing the mom/sister hat by helping Carol when they were outside because Carol had trouble seeing in the bright sunlight.

I had to stand on a wooden crate to reach the cash

register keys. Then as soon as I hit the sum key, I had to jump off the crate, or when the drawer opened—it would knock me off the crate—so I had to jump down and then back up, to make the proper change.

Satisfied customers were always complimenting Mom on her super hamburgers. Although she usually just made hamburgers, I can see her fixing breakfast for travelers, whether it might be a trucker or camper travelers that decided to spend the night in the parking lot.

One day I got off the school bus to quite a surprise. There sat a mini-bus. I was soon to find out what other ideas they were brainstorming. It didn't take them long to have a bright red Coca-Cola cooler with a slide to the side lid for the concession mini-bus. I was to also slide one window of the mini-bus side to side, and to make change in a muffin pan. The only empty corner was stacked with blankets and pillows for my little sisters, to keep them corralled during the drive-in-movie.

Mom popped bags of popcorn for the concession. But first, it was my job to collect twenty-five cents for each car load of people and place the money in a cigar box. Then, I took care of the concession in the mini-bus. I couldn't watch the movies because the lights were strung around the back side of the bus so as not to interfere with the movie. They stretched a screen between two trees.

Dad stopped long enough to deliver the 16" tin that held the canned film before he returned his truck to the company garage. He had built a shelter for the projector to protect it from evening dew. Mom knew how to run the projector, as her family had been projectionists at the movie theatre in Continental for years.

People were very thoughtful though. Before they left, they returned their bottles—and placed them in the empty wooden cases that were left outside the mini-bus. The following morning, my sisters tipped-up every empty bottle, just in case there might be a drop or two left.

The time frame when all this took place was during World War II. Mom's oldest brother had been outside his barracks on Oahu when it was bombed. He was returning home, when his brother was just shipping out. Mom heard that her next brother was killed on Okinawa. Family may have stopped by that Saturday evening, just a short time before she was scheduled to run another film at Pastime Park.

We lived here through a bad winter. We dug tunnels in high drifts. I was in the fourth grade and missed a lot of school that would have to be made up.

I've written about how gossip that has no actual truth or common sense—rebounds like skipping a stone or a golf ball skimming across a narrow water hazard. Either one spreads ripples for yards and yards and yards—but with life, years and years and years.

However, the stories about a 'skirt-chaser' in the same sentence as my Dad, had been observed by numerous family members. I asked one person I trusted in the family, who gently clarified this, "No, you are right. Your Dad was seldom home. He was seeing numerous women then. Not just one in particular."

Now. I have no idea what happened when Mom had finally had enough and was seen in the company of someone other than Dad. For all anyone knew, in broad daylight, she could have just needed someone to talk to.

Of course, this information was quickly shared with Dad. But because I was always the baby-sitter I knew how long she had been gone. But Dad blew his stack. All of a sudden she wasn't being the mother to His Children that he expected. He forced her to leave! Because he had been unfaithful in their marriage—he assumed she was as well?

Dad had replaced Mom with the woman he had been seeing and moved her in. The bedroom didn't have a door on it, just drapes. Well, Susie surprised them the next morning as she drew back the door drapes, and with hands on hips demanded, "What are you doing in my mommy's bed?"

I have no idea how long they planned to stay, however within two weeks, a man representing the courts arrived and asked my sisters and me a lot of questions. This resulted in Mom getting custody of us. I finished the fourth grade in a one-room school while staying with friends of Mom's while she looked for a place to live and a job.

It didn't matter that Dad had chased skirts ninety per cent of the years they had been married. I have no idea what changed her mind—but after their first initial separation family encouraged them to get back together. We moved into a very nice house in Old Fort for a short time until a woman called our house. Mom answered the telephone.

She asked to speak to our Dad. I hid and listened at the top of the entryway stairs.

This other woman claimed she was pregnant, so this was the excuse he used to leave. However no one ever saw a baby but the divorce ensued. My Mom and Dad had a good thing going for them—for us—at Pastime Park, but it didn't matter. There wouldn't be a business without Mom to run it.

I don't know what bothered my Dad more—that she had found someone else, or that he expected her to always be there—waiting. He had been living a double life. That of a married man and a single man.

The divorce happened and once again the courts gave custody of us to our Mom. However, he refused to pay child support. Only recently, I shredded papers from this horrible divorce. It's a past that I wouldn't want to see anyone go through. The second time they went to court isn't worth my time to write about it. Life happens, they say. It was another time, they say. Really?

He made the most noise in the court-room. He had money she did not have. Although several family members offered to take us, they were denied. He demanded if he couldn't have custody of us—then no one could. Odd, but his visits were few at the children's home. His excuse—that we didn't need him. Dad married that 2nd woman and wrote to me that they —meaning her and my Dad—had made mistakes with us girls, but they never offered to make amends.

They would not allow my husband and me to take my sisters out of the children's home and have custody of my sisters. His excuse was that this would be hard on our marriage. And although Mom had been married to George for several years, there was no way he would have allowed them to have custody either. (He had never forgiven our Mom—he had his pride after all.)

This is the reason Mom wanted her daughters to get

an education so they wouldn't get stuck in a marriage with no way out. Especially if children were involved. Strange that she figured out how to run a business by herself.

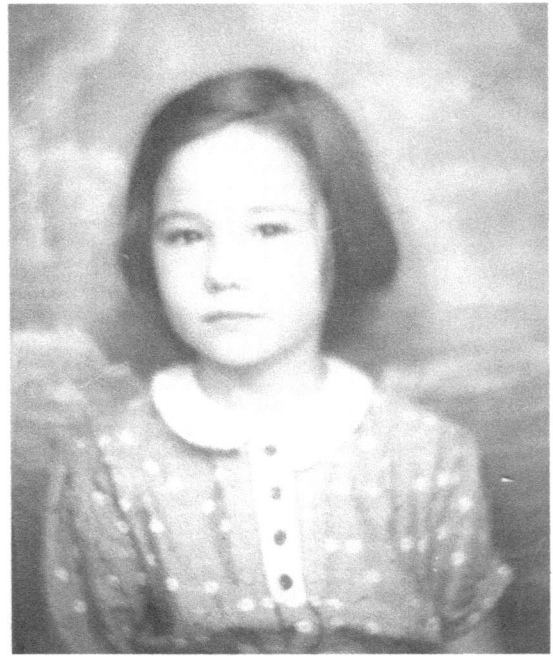

Marilyn, age 7

"The Changing of the Seasons"

The Norwegian Maple Trees
   had weathered yet another
winter—storing energy from
   the sun, snow and rains.
Their sturdy roots clutching
   the soil, expanding their
trunk, yet continued to
   filter carbon dioxide into
life sustaining oxygen.

Due to balmy March
   temperatures, the trees
shivered as brown buds, the
   size of walnuts, exploded;
covering the bare branches.

Despite winters lingering
   snow showers, the buds
finally welcomed April with
   sprouts, in the shape of
spring-green miniature
   umbrellas, that opened
into leaves, offering shelter
   for nesting Robins, a frolicking
squirrel or two—shade and
   cooling summer breezes.

Then cast off encapsulated
   seedlings attached to an

apparent broken wing.
   They drifted, spun,
spiraled to the ground
   like un-manned helicopters.

Summer's leaves were gently
   rocked, tossed and twisted
about due to stormy darkened
   skies, tornado threats, chilling
winds, rain and hail.

Since time began, the seasons
   have been as perennial as
the distance of Earth
   from the Sun.

October's leaves briefly
   became a picturesque,
kaleidoscope painting of
   nature's awesome colors.
Time and temperature cycles
   had weakened their attachment.

Then, November's leaves fell
   silently as snow-flakes.
But when I waded through
   sun-dried, crunching leaves—
it sounded like crumpled
   tissue paper on
Christmas morn.

Our cycle of life in
   comparison: Baby steps
gain confidence, perpetuating
   through the pages of a family's
genealogy—bearing fruit—
   existing to share and leave
behind trails of experience,
   closeness, and a collection of
memories to enrich yet another
   generation. A combination of
their ancestors.

Intro to "The Borrowed Christmas Tree"

The Sunday School Christmas Program
   was over. The fresh-cut Spruce stood at
center stage, still and forlorn, when a
   little girl bravely asked her teacher,
"What happens to the Christmas Tree
   after we go home?"
   "The tree will be burned.
   The decorations packed away."

"Ma'am, please, we won't have a tree this
   year. My little sisters will be sad. They'll
think Santa has forgotten them. Could we
   borrow it for a spell?"

The gruff reply was slow in coming, she
   didn't like this at all.
   "I suppose. But return the decorations
   Sunday next, and leave them in the hall."

"The Borrowed Christmas Tree"

Thus, the Pageant Christmas Tree was just
   on loan for Christmas Eve and Christmas
morn.
   A scattering of snow, barely covered the
ground, helped Santa stop in, no time to roam,
   to leave one doll each for two special little girls.

The dolls waited patiently with perpetual
   smiles, and eyes that never closed. Plus a

Bible Story book signed, from Grandma, for a
girl of eleven was surely too old for dolls.

The dolls could keep secrets, and would never
   tell a soul about the Christmas Eve they arrived,
through ice, and sleet, and snow.

The Christmas Tree stood at attention well lit
   in red, green and gold. The mother bowed her
head in prayer, her heart near overflowed.

The miniature Star of Bethlehem that topped the
   re-born tree, sent shafts of glowing warmth and
surprise in their hearts, joyous with glee.

   Santa's sleigh of dreams and prayers was
stored away until another year. She had faced
   the fearful giant—asked the improbable,
and made her little sisters smile.

Marilyn, Susie, Carol

I was surprised after talking to a writer friend regarding details in an article I was working on. "My memory of 1946 is spot-on about, that nightmare, but memory plays games that are frustrating at times, such as why can I recall most every nook and cranny of Mom's Aunt Hazel's cottage at Islandview, but not one incident at school and only one incident that happened on the school bus. I must have fallen asleep, because I cracked my head on the window of the bus. That woke me up.

I was warned not to tell anyone, or he would come back and kill me and my little sisters. That meant I couldn't even tell Mom. How many nights did I keep that horrible night a secret?

It became even harder, after reading the side of that box my sisters found in Mom's cardboard closet, the day they came out of her bedroom giggling and blowing up these neat skinny balloons. The side of the box read, 'use to prevent pregnancy'!

I was in the 6th grade. 'The what-if screamed in my head that I could have a baby.' But I have to go to school. Years later, I questioned a couple of photos Mom had taken of the three of us. My sisters were wearing dresses with cardigan sweaters, and I am wearing an ankle-length black coat and a dark scarf wrapped around my head. The only thing showing is my face.

Mom knew something was wrong with me, and took me to the doctor. They removed my tonsils and adenoids. What a nice surprise. They gave me a bowl of ice cream after surgery. I had been afraid to go to sleep at night. I must have looked pretty bad, because in a group class picture, I am in the front row due to my height, however, the girl standing beside me spread the skirt of her dress in front of my dress.

When I finally told Mom I saw the profile of the man who had hurt me when her bedroom was flooded with the light of a full moon, as he turned with a glance in the mirrored dresser to adjust his white sailor hat. Fearing that he would find out I had told Mom stole my scratchy voice.

But all I heard was Mom's soft voice, "Lock the front door when I leave—no—hide in the basement. I won't be gone long," she whispered. We didn't have a phone, but it was like she had lost her voice. When she returned, she said, "We're leaving tonight."

We packed in cardboard boxes and stuffed pillow cases. Her silence was like a contagious disease. Mom had found another house for us, until I finished school. Later, a daytime job and the ideal place, because the lady who lived in a little mobile home was just a few steps from the porch of the house Mom had rented, and she could babysit us while Mom was at work.

It was relaxing sitting on the porch swing. Just a few weeks later, all our lives were about to change forever. We were admitted to the Allen County Children's Home for six weeks. After the divorce was final, Seneca County, Ohio Children's Services drove us to our next residence, the Flat Rock Children's Home.

I started to feel safe after overhearing a conversation between one of the senior girls and a newbie a year or so younger than me ask, "Why don't you lock the doors? Aren't you afraid someone might break in here?"

"Why in the world would someone break in here, when most of us would like to leave?" That made sense to me.

By then, being an observer, I had learned to keep good and bad to myself. I had never acted in either of our school plays, but pretense became my middle name. Don't let them see you cry or care—which came in handy when Father A. berated me because my grades didn't suit him, when he said, "You want to end up like your parents?" His growling voice sounded like he had a nasty taste in his mouth.

I could still remember, as an eight-year-old, how I made change inside the Pastime Park Restaurant and when I handled all sales inside the movie concession bus. My parents were business savvy—they just didn't score well when it came to marriage. Keeping all of this to myself meant being a survivor.

One thing I was really proud of in the seventh grade at Thompson School was, I received my first A in addition to Spelling, since grammar school. I drew the best and most accurate, dandy, larger-then-life, beautiful grasshopper on the blackboard. My drawing was the only one our teacher left on the blackboard all week.

"A Full Moon Reflected"

A full 1946 moon reflected
   off the midnight water—
Mom was late getting
   home from work…

He picked me up, to put
   this eleven year-old to bed,
but his intentions were
   for his satisfaction.

The stranger left me in
   horrifying shame with
a lifetime nightmare of
   my stolen innocence.

He breathed a warning.
   'Don't tell anyone or I
will be back and kill
   your little sisters & you!'

I stood beside the
   black water's edge.
No man would
   marry me now.

Considered dying—
   but the Lord's
message was clear,
   your sisters need you.

I finally told Mom. Nailed
　the windows shut.
Placed the hammer
　close to the door.

Until we moved, I slept
　between my sisters,
my arms around
　them all night.

We moved again. This house-
　rent included an on-site
babysitter. Surely possible
　on a waitress's income.

Because Dad was so far
　behind on child support,
Children's Services filed -
　but he turned the table

to his advantage, and he
　and his mother contacted
Children's Services—saying
　his children were alone.

So. While Mom was at work,
　these strangers insisted we
had to leave with them. I had no
　way of contacting Mom.

It was only Dad's lies,
   and Children's Services
word for what happened that
   day. I have no memory of it!

After Mom died quite
   young, my sisters and I
contacted Children's Services.
   Their file revealed that I

wasn't very cooperative.
   No kidding! I failed Mom
and my sisters. Mom arrived
   home to find her girls gone.

My sisters and I were delivered
   to the Allen County Children's
Home for six weeks. When the
   Courts and Dad were finished,

we had become Wards of the Court.
   Seneca County Children's Services
Reps. drove us to the Flat Rock Ebenezer
   Evangelical United Brethren Children's
Home in Flat Rock.

"The Velveteen Steel River"

The once fragile bits—and—
   pieces of my life had been
molded into velveteen steel.
   But when a bold headline

reported another had been
   sentenced to a few years in prison
for the number of children
   they had physically used—

every time—captured my attention
   and sent me down the
rewind trail of the
   strangely painful silence—

to a place where my innocent
   heart and mind survived. Was
this what others had possibly
   wished for? Needed perhaps?

Likened to patched pot-holes,
   and buried memories—my
thank-you-prayers, and good-
   riddance goodbye to

the shadowed nightmares.
   Salty rain washed away
into the river of relief,
   and over the bridge

of smooth asphalt, titled
  "the possibility of closure,"
to courageously believe it's
  safe to love and be loved?

Whenever the reminder
  caught me unaware,
his arms were always
  my safe haven.

Don's patient condolences
  smoothed the stricken
shivering in my trembling
  heart as I struggled to

understand how the immoral,
  got off their disgusting
jollies taking advantage of the
  disadvantaged and children,

who are left frightened, and
  embarrassed, like my
nightmare stranger who got
  off scot free, because he could.

Whereas in an adult
  relationship—there are
expectations, rules, love,
  honesty. Not free-for the
taking, and the word NO!!!

"Keys"

Do all doors
  need a key?
An unassuming
  reason to be?

From opening
  the door
to your
  heart—

to the
  enticing
cover of
  a book—

treasured memories
  your home
your car
  the Pearly Gates?

Yet, keys of
  patience
prayer
  possibility

however, might
  just challenge you—
or at the very least
  keep you safe

from
  the uninvited,
unexpected,
  unknown.

Susie, Marilyn, Carol (Lima)

"The Children's Home Wake Up and Wiggle Bell"
First published in the Enterprise, *December 18, 1989*

In 1947, the bell rang and echoed across
   the halls, the well-manicured lawn,
and nearby, in the sleeping town,
   ordering all who weren't up to get up!

Girls from five to seventeen,
   in their cottage, three stories high,
big and little boys in theirs,
   bobbed up—rubbing their
still sleep-filled eyes.

Each made their dorm beds,
   eight, twelve beds to a row.
Pajama clad, bare feet, little girls
   dashed across the cold oak floor

into their respective dressing rooms
   to quickly shed pajamas—they
scrambled into cotton print dresses
   and sweater, the boys in jeans
and sturdy oxford shoes. Clattering

feet clumped down the well-worn
   concrete stairs, second of three
flights to the basement below, to wait
   their turn for one of the two

bathroom stalls. In the wash room,
 they elbowed their turn at one of the
sinks, to brush their teeth, comb their
 hair, wash their face and hands;

drying on his or her own numbered
 towel pegged numerically in a row.
The matron clapped her hands when
 the second bell tolled one ding-dong
clear and sweet—it's time to eat.

Softly murmuring, the girls walked
 slowly hand-in-hand through
the connecting archway to the
 Main Building at seven a.m.
The boys filed in smelling
 of crisp air and wool.

Breakfast time in the cheery dining
 room, tables set to serve eighty.
Little and big girls and boys,
 workers and matrons, as well,
filed in and stood silently
 behind their assigned chairs.

The piano player's introduction
 hummed the first verse of a hymn
for all to sing. Chairs slid,
 skidded and bumped—
all were silently seated.

Father read morning worship
    From the Upper Room,
Followed by a prayer.

Juice was sipped. Milk was
    poured. Breakfast bowls were
passed. Excitement bubbled. The
    children's eyes glistened.

Christmas was in the air.
    The brightly lit ten foot
evergreen filled the large room
    with the scent of pine,
expectancy and dreams.
    Promising Santa's arrival
that Christmas Eve.

Christmas Eve, Santa and his
    helpers stopped at each cottage,
dragged in large bags and boxes
    of bundles wrapped in brown
paper, tied with cord—each
    taped with a name printed
boldly across. Then each child
    waited until all had a gift.

On cue—pandemonium,
   torn paper and surprise!
Only Santa knew Mother had
shopped all-year-round to fill
   her store room shelves;
then scurried the month
   before to find a special request
listed in each 'Santa Letter'.

Each bundle consisted of: new
   socks, undies, nylon hose, a
shirt, blouse or sweater, hat or
   gloves, toothbrush and comb,
books, crayons, games, toy trucks
   dolls, model cars or planes,
lipstick, lotion, cologne,
   after shave.

Each item was carefully noted,
   admired, then shelved in
personal lockers, closets or
   drawers. This night, each child
felt someone cared.

"A Summer Morning"

The morning sun
   awakens another new day
to glisten and sparkle
   like precious jewels,

on the swaying branches,
   gentle leaves, tiny blades
of grass to broad leaves
   in a field of corn.

This gentleness is
   God's time. The
morning, just after
   a sweet sunrise.

A time to remember.
   A time to plan.
To start another day,
   and set cares aside—

to savor each precious
   moment to thank You,
God for another day, for
   the strength and

patience, that I
   can fulfill your
expectations,
   and plans for me.

My first pair of high heels was in 1950. The Flat Rock Children's Home evening meal was interrupted by the waitress's chimes. Silence filled the dining room as Father A. stood. I had yet to calm the jitters from ruining Sunday dinner when, while adding more milk to the three/quarter bushel of mashed potatoes in the floor mixer with a glass pitcher—it slipped from my hands. It wasn't my first time. I could weigh ingredients for four 8x10 cake pans and have them in the oven in less than 20 minutes.

I had been horrified. Mother was always preaching about not wasting food. Plus, I worried about what could replace the potatoes and what punishment would follow later. But he stood and announced, "There will be no mashed potatoes for dinner as planned, however the waiters will be serving more bread and gravy to each table within a few minutes."

I was still so upset that I almost missed the second part of his announcement. "I will be in the Store Room for anyone needing shoes replaced or repaired on the second floor, down the hall from Nurse Witt's Medical Station from 7:00 till 8:30 p.m. tomorrow evening."

I had outgrown my everyday and school/church shoes. When I walked into the Store Room I couldn't believe my eyes. Even before I took a seat to wait my turn, I spotted the most beautiful pair of shoes that were anything but practical. I crossed my fingers, praying no one ahead of me wanted that pair of red high heeled shoes. Plus, they looked like they would fit.

I start high school in the fall. I know I can't wear them to school, I thought, *but I could wear them to church.* Grinning from ear to ear changed to challenging disbelief, but I was so choked up, my voice came out in a whisper when I realized he had heard even that.

"You know Mother and I noticed you have been hobbling around in shoes you have out-grown for weeks. Speak up. No one is going to do it for you. You have a pair of every-day shoes, a pair for school and church, and what about those red high-heeled shoes? "

"If I try them on and they fit—may I borrow them as well?"

He nodded and proceeded to repair a pair of shoes one of the little boys had brought in.

I couldn't wait to get to the Big Girls' Cottage where I practiced walking around in them, from the floral living room carpet, to the hard-wood floor in the study, to the noisy click, click, click, on the white marble-like bath-room floor. No matter how many times I adjusted the buckle at my ankles, my big and second toe stuck through the open-toed part of the shoes.

I liked the idea of appearing to be almost five feet tall since I would be starting high school in the fall. Thankfully, Mom had bought me one pair of hose, which I had hidden away so no one would know I had them. Keeping my nails snag-free would be as daily a chore as brushing my teeth—between washing pots and pans after every meal, and the cleaning of the floor to ceiling white cupboards the length of the kitchen every Saturday.

Sunday morning, every step I took clicked along, even though I was being careful where the tree roots had raised the sidewalk in sections angled uphill, and downhill, plus I needed to be careful to miss the cracks that the heels could get caught in, like car tires could get caught in pot holes on the highway.

If my feet could talk, they would question my sanity putting them through such torture. My big toes were aimed towards the ground, however my arches felt like they were being bombarded by imaginary huge marbles, and my ankles struggled through a twisty balancing dance act.

Of course the boys were whistling and making comments like 'la-tee-da. Aren't we fancy!' It was a good thing I could lean against the trees that were close-by once in a while. This row

of Ash Trees had been planted in the yard-wide grassy area between the road and the sidewalk, and the distance from the edge of the children's home front lawn to the church. The boys liked to tell the story about how special these trees were because their wood was used for baseball-bats.

I had usually kept my distance from the older girls in the cottage; however, they apparently knew before I did that I was still missing a very important garment, a garter belt to fasten my hose to.

However, while I was writing a letter to Mom asking her for one, one of the older girls asked me to join her in the dressing room. Using their collection of borrowed safety pins the senior girls took tucks in the borrowed belt until it fit me. They also taught me how to carefully put on and remove my hose, and most importantly, where to clip the top of my hose to the belt.

After I stood still in the church choir loft and sat down during the sermon, managing the stairs back down to hang up my choir robe was easier, although I still used the handrails.

I soon outgrew these heels. They were a size 4-1/2, the same size my mom wore. One of the older girls said when they grew-up, they were going to wear bobby-socks with their high heels like my Mom did. I do not believe this was stylish in the fifties.

Just goes to show the next time something catches my eye, it might be best to analyze what looks like an exciting prospect may not be so interesting after all.

However, it didn't stop me from breaking-in a brand new pair of black spike heels, square-dancing years later.

Marilyn, new skirt

Stream of consciousness

Lavender blossoms fresh delicate scent haunts the heart in layers of blue acetate in a world painted in lavender, enchanting, a moment between the black of night and the blushing rose, into candlelight gold, dissipating into the colorless light of day observe, search, feel, reach out, absorb as hearts and minds become one on a similar path to reveal thoughts sent through time runs all barricades into infinity.

Messages not new, but renewed with changes in guidelines, in style in stratosphere man is one in God, one in thought, one in being. An unchanging picture of kindness, tenderness, fury, futility, fairness, finesse open to thought mutely shared, its elusiveness when indelibly caressed cannot fade, but returns, repeats, remains forever held in Lavender, the beginning of this circle of time.

Reverend Acres, a Children's Home 1951 employee, had dropped us off at a distant church for a District Youth Fellowship meeting in the nine-passenger children's home black Buick; nicknamed the 'hearse'. Several hours later, an employee at the children's home, arrived to pick us up in the five-passenger children's home backup vehicle. When he pulled up, he said, "John, why don't you sit in front with me where there is more leg room."

It had started to sprinkle when I clambered into the back seat. Not easy to do in my favorite yellow suit, even though the skirt was calf-length and slightly flared. I was surprised that J.R. had beat me to the corner seat. Apparently the mechanic had fixed the other rear passenger door.

There he sat with one arm up on the back of the seat. When I looked up, he winked at me with those mysterious blue eyes, plus a charming shy smile to boot. The administration forbids dating except for the Junior/Senior Prom, so what was he thinking?

Midway across the seat, my skirt had started to twist around my legs. Ladylike be hanged, with one foot on either side of the hump on the floor, I raised up just enough to straighten my skirt and plopped ungraciously very close to J.R. Then, his sister, Mary and John's sister, Jeannie, said teasingly, "Hurry up. Scooch over. We're getting wet!"

It isn't like I didn't know who J.R. was. We had eaten in the same dining room three times every day, and attended church twice a week for over three years. However, when school started my sophomore year, he had started sitting beside me on the school bus a few times a week. He never asked, *Mind if I sit here?* but then he totally ignored me anyhow. Then it finally dawned on me. No wonder! He was interested in a gorgeous blonde across the aisle.

When the car doors closed, it was instantly dark in the back seat. I hadn't been this close to anyone, except Nurse Gracie when she had taped closed my leg when I misjudged the height of a stack of apple crates. Even when mom visited, she never hugged me—but usually hugged my two little sisters.

Reverend Lucas and John were talking about engines and the girls beside me were chattering about making some new friends. I couldn't think of a thing to say because the feelings I was caught-up in were so new and scrambled on auto-pilot.

The windshield wipers and tires were so rhythmic and soothing that at any other time I would have fallen asleep like the girls beside me had. But I was wide awake!

Then J.R. gently squeezed my shoulder and whispered, "Are you comfortable?" When had his hand gotten so close to my shoulder? I had left more than one guy with scratches on their arms for making unwanted, and sometimes unexpected passes. But J.R. touching my shoulder didn't feel wrong.

Comfortable? No. I wanted to reply. Why was he acting like he liked me, or was he just flirting with me? He had removed his jacket before he got in the car. Why, when the hair on his arm touched my neck, did I feel like a cloud of butterflies had joined that piece of fluffy lemon meringue pie I had eaten earlier.

I turned my head to answer him when his lips breezed past my cheek at the same time that J.R. and John suddenly yelled, "The tracks!"

Apparently, the Reverend had been distracted and forgot to slow down for the hilled-up railroad crossing. I'm certain we went airborne at the speed he was driving. We landed with a thud so hard on the other side of the tracks that the Reverend's hat was scrunched flat from hitting the roof of the car. The rear bench seat had slid forward and we went with it. Rev. Lucas was distraught, and yelled, "Is everyone back there okay?"

"Not quite, Reverend," J.R. replied. "John and I will have to get out of the car and shove the seat back in place."

J.R. had wrapped his arms around me so tight I could barely breathe, but quickly released me and asked, "Were you hurt?"

I replied, "No." But barely recognized my own voice, and thought, 'I had forgotten what a hug felt like. I could feel his heart beat when my ear was pressed against his chest.'

Mary was against the other door and whimpered that her arm hurt, and her foot was caught between the front and back seats.

Thankfully the rain had stopped and everyone was subdued the rest of the way home. Whether anyone had seen J.R.'s moves or first-practice maybe-kiss, the unwritten code of silence now included the Reverend.

I had overheard the older girls talk about sneaking out and that for generations, guys visited the Big Girls Cottage—dating after hours. But nothing about a racing heart beat as a result of a brush of his lips on my cheek? Anyhow, I barely felt his interrupted butterfly touch attempt.

However, two weeks later while walking back to the home after youth fellowship followed by Sunday night church service, J.R. caught my hand in his and we walked side by side. We weren't even allowed to be talking together. But with him holding my hand in his, it had been so long since anyone had even touched me, but I felt a different connection I didn't know had been missing in my life. Trust. I felt safe.

Then smoothly as a dance move, he stopped and gently guided me behind one of the numerous Ash trees that lined the route, in the grassy area between the sidewalk and the road. Fog had settled in the nearby corn field during the evening service. The air was a bit chilly, but with his coat open, and his hands against the tree on either side of me—I was suddenly warm in a cocoon of his making.

"I've been wanting to do this forever," he said softly, as he backed up momentarily and then held my face in his hands. The look in his eyes was mesmerizing. "No surprises this time," he added. The kiss was warm and gentle, but then it seemed when I responded—how could I not—he pulled away. I recognized reluctance in his eyes.

I think I had forgotten to breathe. On another level the fear that Father might decide to do a drive-by was stone-cold reality. J.R. tapped me on the nose and smiled—then added softly, "I've got to see you. I will be in touch," and he ran ahead to catchup with the other guys.

It had all happened so fast, and I had yet to move when his older sister approached me and said, "Come along now or we'll be late getting in."

That cleared my head. The fog cooled my cheeks. But the memory of my first real kiss lingered for a lifetime. I was just 15, going on 16.

"Lavender—Rose & Marigold Lace"

Still wrapped in
  memories of the past
hopefully building a
  future yet unknown,

lavender blossoms'
  fresh delicate scent
haunts hearts in
  layers of blue.

As friendship culminates
  into anticipation—
and unexpected
  connections linger,

the blushing rose
  blossoms into
surprising second-
  chance-choices

 in thoughtful
contemplation
  and framed
in marigold lace.

While I was working in the Children's Home kitchen in 1951—1952, I was just finishing my half of Saturday's weekly cleaning schedule when Mother stopped by and asked if I would like to help her sort through the most recent boxes of donations that had just arrived.

I smiled, pleased she had asked and replied, "Yes." I locked up the kitchen, and prayed no one would sneak in and steal some of the chocolate cake I had baked today for Sunday's evening meal.

The last time she had invited me to try on clothes, she gave me a yellow satin 8"x 10" holder that had the word HANKIES across the front with the picture of a lady dressed in black lace Flapper Days outfit. I now had something to store my hankies in.

When I joined her in the store room, she commented, "You are outgrowing your blouses. Try a couple of these on as well. She didn't mention a new bra, but placed it on top of the blouses. I thought at the time, so this is what one calls an unmentionable?

I felt my face turn shades of pink as I gathered them in my arms, including a nice dress for church, and went into the nearby bathroom for privacy. I knew the routine. I was expected to try them on and get her approval to see how they fit. I would be a sophomore when school started in the fall.

Then for Christmas I received a brand new, store bought, not second hand, white sweater. I was so excited to receive such a lovely sweater to wear to school after the

Christmas Holidays. This was the first time my sisters and I would have family we were allowed to stay overnight with over Christmas.

I never did find out how one of Dad's sisters managed that. She picked us up, and the best part was our aunt had invited Mom and step-dad, as well. Our first Christmas with Mom since we had arrived at the Children's Home. I was excited to wear my new sweater. I also knew I would wash it by hand, after seeing what happened when one of the girls tossed one of her sweaters in the regular laundry and it had come back a miniature of itself.

I couldn't wait to wear this very special soft white sweater to school. After lunch and just before study hall, three upper class girls approached me. I was sitting in my seat when they leaned over me and warned, "Don't you dare wear that sweater to school anymore! The boys are looking at you and ignoring us!"

My first thought was, *The boys are looking at me—that way? Oh, no.* I never went to the bathroom by myself ever again after one of the boys in my class jumped at me out of the shadows and grabbed at my chest. Thank heavens I had on my boyfriend's FFA Jacket which was loose around my shoulders. But I ran up the stairs as fast as I could go and never told a soul.

I never wore a sweater to school again. I wore them to church and since I was in choir- we wore robes that covered my sweaters and I felt more comfortable standing straight with my shoulders back as directed by our choir director.

Years later, I was shopping with a daughter when a young man stood staring at a table of lady's unmentionables, like he was on another planet. Then he looked up at me and shyly asked, "Ma'am, my wife and I just had a baby and she asked me to buy her a new bra. You're built a lot like my wife—so which one of these would you buy?"

I found my size in the section of boxed bras and handed it to him. I thought there was no way my husband would have ventured into the ladies department, period.

"Christmas News 2004"

Happy thoughts race
   through my mind.
Just won't leave me
   alone, till I take the

time, to quickly jot
   down the mysterious,
the master of creating
   pretense, in the space

where only facts and
   dates abound. Turn
the pages of time to
   contemplate yourself
in the memories.

The day the study room on the big girls' side of the Girls' Cottage in August 1952 took on a new meaning was the day Mother B. stomped up the stairs and ordered all the girls to join her in our study.

Of course, there was no way any of us ever knew what bee she had in her bonnet when she showed up out of the blue. She was known to search through our dressers, our closets, wherever she pleased.

She walked over towards the windows where our sewing machine sat and called me to join her. No. I had not seen the wooden paddle she had hidden in the folds of her dress. She stared at me and said, "Come over here. Now. Did you steal that spice from the kitchen?"

I replied, as I had earlier in the kitchen, "No. Matron R. asked me to borrow it for her."

Matron R. stood there with the other girls and said nothing.

"Matron R. said she did not ask you to get that spice for her. So. Now, you own up to the truth. Just admit that you were stealing that spice from the Children's Home Kitchen!" Mother B. demanded. "Admit you are lying!"

Again, I shook my head no. I recognized the spice tin as having belonged to a former cook who had acquired a taste for a south-western style casserole which she must have kept and possibly ate in her room. I believe she stopped by the kitchen to warm it up, and I was still there because it had been a Saturday, which was cleaning day on my side of the kitchen.

"Bend over," she demanded, as she bent me over the back of the sewing machine chair, she flipped my dress up, and whacked me with the wooden paddle, so hard I gripped the rungs of the back of the chair. I had never felt so humiliated in my entire life.

I lost count of the number of times she demanded, and I shook my head no, and said, "No."

I could see Matron R.'s feet, and she stood there the entire time, and never said a word. I knew she cooked on her hot plate in her apartment which was against the rules.

The administrators trusted me with the keys to the kitchen. Mother B. knew I had no need to steal the stupid spice that was so old the tin was rusty. If I had wanted to use it, I had access to it. Thus whatever she thought she was going to accomplish by whipping me, I still have no idea.

Suddenly the room got quiet. She left me there. When I heard the archway door close behind her clopping down the stairs, I cautiously straightened-up, pushed my dress down and hid behind the hallway door in a corner. I never cried. I just gripped my stomach gently where my body had been shoved into the back of the chair. Why she beat me that day, I will never know.

The anger, at least, lost out to the pain. There was no way I could have ridden my bicycle. I did go to the kitchen and helped with the evening meal, and did the kitchen pots and pans, and cleanup as usual, but I didn't eat in the dining room. However, someone fixed me something to eat before I finished in the kitchen.

This happened in the summer, two weeks before my senior year in high school started. I had to deal with both of these women until graduation. I have never been a good actress but I soon realized neither of these women would ever apologize. I would have to be on my best behavior, or my two younger sisters would pay for this mess after I left.

I did such a good job pretending that until I started describing this Study Room in detail for this memoir was this happening unearthed. Which was followed by why Mother B. asked me to help her decorate the Main Building Dining Room huge Christmas tree. She never allowed anyone to assist decorating this tree. These were her personal decorations. Then a week or so later, she invited me to help her wrap Christmas gifts for the children. No one had ever heard of her asking anyone do that, either. I never questioned why she gave me carte-blanch when I suggested meals we only served on special occasions.

I was stunned when Matron R. gave me a necklace with matching earrings for a graduation gift. However every time I looked at them I couldn't bring myself to wear them. I refused to allow the remembrance to sour the love I had for my husband, loving children and friends.

Of course I didn't handle this by myself. I Thanked the Lord for the chance to put something like this in the past—to give me the strength to pretend I had forgotten it. Like a scar that leaves its mark, the lesson not to ever take out my frustrations on any innocent bystander, when I have run across a 'why' I couldn't find the answer to. Yes. I believe I wore out the tires on that bicycle when the past would sneak up on me when I least expected.

Although I couldn't take my sisters with me, graduation couldn't come soon enough.

"A Novel Story and Muse"

As a story
   emerges from a
picture seared
   in our memory

it is enhanced
   with imagination—
passion, surprising
   destination and—

foreshadowed
   with intriguing
clues, plus—
   challenging conflicts.

However, ingredients
   for a story are also
in the research,
   the details—

and, determining
   who did what, why,
why not, when,
where and how—

one must combine
   unwavering focus,
discipline, belief
   and prayer that
you too can
   conquer this
electrifying
   journey.

"A Collection Of Memories"
First published in The Senior's Beacon for the 55 & Older *in 1987*

Dear Main Building,
   You were built in 1868, by the
      Ebenezer Flat Rock Church
         for children orphaned
            by the Civil War.

Always a lady, your walls kept our secrets,
   echoed our laughter and tears, yet
      gave shelter, warmth and love
         to homeless children
            through the years.

Left forgotten, the blizzard of 1978,
   shattered your windows, burst frozen pipes,
      buckled once cared for wooden floors,
         and left you standing, three stories tall,
            serene, deserted, destroyed from within.

Then, mid-year 1981, your white brick walls
   were leveled, and left a collection
      of memories in an empty
         space, spring scented with
            lily of the valley and rose.

Choices. Goals. Dreams.

Only the high-school students who had the top grades were chosen to attend four-year college prep meetings, thus I thought there was no need to even consider college. It was the spring of 1952 with 1953 on my mind, when I was sitting in a doctor's office because our children's home nurse allowed me to accompany Donna, a children's home sister, while she had her physical in preparation to attend nursing school after graduation.

While waiting for Donna, I was curious why others were there to see the doctor. Usually, he came to the children's home to give us flu shots at our nurse's station. When a lovely elderly lady walked in with the grace of a dancer, smiled in my direction, drew a handkerchief scattered with pink roses printed on it, and proceeded to pat moisture from her forehead and the back of her neck.

She had such poise, I felt certain she must be a model, or at least had money because the fabric and style of her dress surely had been top of the line by a famous designer. "Are you waiting to see the doctor?" she asked.

"No." I replied. "One of my friends is seeing the doctor. She plans to become a nurse."

"That's a very good career. What do you plan to do?"

"Others think I would do well as a model because I have the best posture in our class."

She looked me over and said, "You are not thin enough, or possibly tall enough. I have treated young women who starved themselves to meet the rare qualifications. You might consider a different career."

I took her advice and liked the idea of a business college. I enjoyed short-hand, typing and bookkeeping, and finally had a plan. I knew that my dad and children's services and the children's home administration could have forced me to stay at the children's home until I turned eighteen.

Thus, after a Greyhound Bus trip to Lima, I signed up for classes that started just a week after graduation. I left the night of high-school graduation with Mom and step-dad, George. I left the children's home world of insulation to a world of responsibility. A world where clothes and meals were furnished to a world where one was required to work to earn the funds to pay to ride the city bus, to pay for a root beer or cola, a sandwich, a winter coat, notebooks and pencils. Thanks to Mom and my step-dad, I had free room and board.

Mom had set up an interview with the owners of the Big Wedge on Findlay Road/Flanders in Lima. I felt they hired me after I explained I had worked in the children's home kitchen, and had four years of grill experience, and helping the cook, cook for 80 people.

I wouldn't turn eighteen until October, thus I wasn't permitted to work after nine o'clock P.M. Then one weekend, two waitresses called in sick and I was asked to work. When the Saturday night Robin Hood Dance Hall let out, there was an influx of customers ordering breakfast.

There was a picture that has never left my memory. That of a very pregnant mid-twenties inebriated woman, flanked with a man on either side of her. She was giggling as each of the men cuddled her like she belonged to both of them. They all sounded and acted like they needed food and lots of black coffee before they left the parking lot.

The next time Mom stopped in at the Big Wedge for a cup of coffee, I overheard one of the regulars stop Mom and say, "If I ever see your daughter working here after nine o'clock, I will report you." But the lesson I learned that evening was how alcohol could affect a person's common sense.

After a practice run, Mom had left me on my own with bus tokens to ride the city bus to the Dominion Building on East High Street, just off North Main. Northwestern School of Commerce was on the 2nd floor. This may have been the first time I had ever rode in an elevator.

I rode the city bus to downtown Lima, Monday through Friday, from the Findlay Road stop at a grocery across from the Adams Street stop. At a Flanders stop, a woman my age stepped aboard the bus. There wasn't one empty seat. One man to a seat throughout. Two women sitting together and I was sitting by myself. I motioned for her to join me. She smiled and breathed a sigh of relief. We became fast friends. She was living with her grandfather and was working at an attorney's office in downtown Lima.

Coffee was cheaper than a soda. And I hadn't become accustomed to pasteurized whole milk that tasted like colored water. I had been used to fresh from the farm, real milk. Coffee was a nickel and a grilled ham-salad sandwich was twenty-cents—cheaper than a quarter Kewpie hamburger.

Mrs. Jules Barnett, wife of the owner of Northwestern School of Commerce, was our teacher in office equipment, proper dress and office etiquette. The proper dress was just an extension of the children's home administrator, wherein we had to pass inspection before getting on the school bus each morning.

It was exciting to sit in a class where everyone was planning a career. I never missed a day of school. I had great respect for those who had returned from battles in war zones, sitting in class across the aisle from me. Mom's one brother was on Oahu when it was bombed and one of her brothers was killed on Okinawa during WWII.

After class, the city bus made a special stop at the Big Wedge for me. I studied when I took my break and ate whatever I was allowed for my evening meal, which was greatly appreciated. However, the employees would not allow me to walk the four blocks home by myself. There weren't any street lights for one thing. But there weren't any sidewalks either. It was a main highway.

It was a surprising Sunday and the Big Wedge was packed except for two seats at the counter, when a black couple entered and were seated. They were a very gracious, nicely dressed middle-aged couple. I took their order and was preparing their drinks, when I was told, "You will serve them on paper plates instead of china."

This was a first of this type of order, but it only took me a moment to understand, and I replied, "I will not serve them on paper plates. Your cook uses her hands to handle the lightest, most delicious biscuits for miles around. And you have a black girl washing and drying dishes people eat on."

When I placed their meals in front of them, a table of six from out of state left—even though their dinners were ready to serve. Then a young man came back and laid a silver dollar on the table and said, "Sorry. I'm just a passenger."

Months later, my bus-riding friend, Pat and her fiancée introduced me to his best friend from high school, who had just returned home after serving in the Army in Korea and Japan. I was off-work and waiting at the Big Wedge to meet them, knowing they were stopping after a high-school basketball game.

I had learned to be cautious, because when I was introduced to the mother of a couple of previous dates, the mothers didn't even try to hide their dislike of me. Odd. That growing up in a children's home had a different connation compared to a private school—which is where Mom's mom told people her granddaughters were.

However, when I met Don's parents, they accepted me from day one. I was touched by the love and respect I observed between him and his parents. It was something I had been looking for. Was happiness really possible?

Marilyn & Don

"A Master Plan"

New Beginnings
   aren't just a New Year,
a new month, a new week,
   a new day, a new moment—

and new isn't always
   never tried, first time,
first born, or re-born
   but caught on a

disheartening precipice,
   until discovering
paths well-traveled,
   for the healing of a
bruised and nostalgic spirit.

New Beginnings of
   this year's visions
are strengthened by
   yesteryear's growth,

and lessons learned, which
   can spring you forward with
a compassionate heart
   and a gleam in your eye.

New Beginnings inscribed
   Believe! You must believe
you are still here for a reason.
   Thankfully shoulder the

expectations. Humbly capture
   memories of the unexpected,
and welcome the surprises, as
   God's Master Plan unfolds.

Sometimes, everyone needs someone who, without hesitation, makes them feel special and loved. "Just hold me," I cried and Don did just that—many times, over the years. This isn't something I planned.

There were times when I was just plain tired. I sat on his lap, and curled up in his arms whenever I had really had a bad day. This could have even been an argument with one of our children, especially those conversations that felt we left unsolved.

There are some mixed messages about dealing with challenges—one of those 'darned if you do and darned if you don't'. And, you choose your battles carefully, which usually resulted in 'pray they calm down and use their common sense'.

Sometimes, it was because of my own insecurity—wondering if and when he would find someone who was really smart, beautiful, a better homemaker, and had a regular income. Few marriages lasted anyhow right?

I had worked as a secretary/receptionist outside the home, even after my first child was born, however I wanted to be a stay-at-home parent. As soon as Don had a more stable job, I could do just that. Anyhow, I felt my extensive garden and preserving an average of one-hundred quarts of fruit and vegies a year, made a big percentage of our children's clothes and gifts, more than equaled a paycheck.

But of course, I didn't have a paycheck. However, the costs to work outside the home would have required: the costs of a car, purchase a new wardrobe, pay for childcare, plus replace the groceries I would have had in my garden, and our children would be coming home from school to an empty house.

However, my writing changed my outlook. It gave me more confidence in myself. Of course I gave a lot of credit to Don and his mom and dad because they accepted me from day one.

Then something that doesn't come up in everyday conversations, I noticed the interaction between Don's parents who had raised eleven children, that there was still a loving gentleness between the two of them. At eighty years old, they had been doing dishes. She was washing and he was drying, when he put his arm around her, kissed her on the cheek and whispered something to her. She blushed and they both smiled.

Of course, this was a special moment. I had never seen this type of interaction between couples that was so beautiful. I was standing on the porch waiting for Don to join me when he just opened the screen door and we went in.

Weeks later he was in this same kitchen trying on new outfits, when I felt drawn to him, and wanted to be alone with him. I had a feeling that not only surprised but embarrassed me. My face felt flushed and yet how could I know what this feeling was supposed to feel like?

Later, when I told him how I felt, he just chuckled. I never felt it was wrong or bad, but I had felt this emotional connection when our eyes met and when we held hands, my heart caught and I felt it had skipped a beat or two. How could all this bring tears?

I had never felt like this when other guys had kissed

me, nor felt truly loved like this before, but he treated me like I was really special, that he really cared.

We decided to get baptized on Easter Sunday at the Methodist Church in Lima, where two of his sisters were members. Three of his other siblings were baptized that day too. This was a very special weekend because Don had asked me to marry him the night before.

"Alone?"

Alone. Alone? Yes, alone.
   At some time, aren't we all?
Alone with our thoughts
   never to be shared.

Alone gentle heart—once-
   broken for another
I once cared. But
   alone with the Lord

where safety abounds.
   Alone dear heart where
lost love and tears
   makes it's rounds.

Alone to its aching depths
   I really can't share,
alone and hidden from view
   protecting me unaware?

Alone must I forever stay
   with this heart once-broken?
Alone—pray—pray not forever.
   Your smile touched my heart.

Set it free. Alone?
   Not now.
We're together.
   You and me.

I stood in the alcove of Irene's Dress Shop on Elizabeth Street in Lima, Ohio, admiring the lovely powder blue dress in the display window. What was I thinking?

The lady I had replaced, had resigned because she was expecting her first baby and was planning to be a stay-at-home mom. Then she changed her mind, and wanted her job back. Just when my boss and I figured out how his new dictation machine worked. I knew shorthand!

Wow! My first secretarial job after graduating from business-college certainly didn't last very long. I wasn't fired, just replaced and let-go. But at least the owner felt bad and gave me a one-hundred dollar bonus. That was a lot of money in 1954 especially since I didn't even have a job.

I had noticed this unusual dress in the window, every time I had passed Irene's Bridal Shop for weeks. Taking a deep breath, I stepped inside and was greeted by, "How may I help you?"

I thought of all the things I could spend that much money on, and replied, "I am getting married in six weeks. I love the blue dress in the window," which I assumed was meant as a bridesmaid's dress, "But all I have to spend is one-hundred dollars."

After I tried it on, the sales lady suggested, "It fits you nicely." I frowned when I noted the gown was strapless, except for a blue velvet strap over one shoulder. Noticing my hesitation she suggested. "We can make a blue lace shrug and order blue veil fabric from New York, add a small crown for your veil, plus tax, and keep it all within your one-hundred dollar budget."

I paid for the dress, and before I gave it a second thought, I stopped by another shop and used my emergency twenty for a powder blue nightgown that reached my ankles for $19.95.

Expecting my mom to put up a fuss, similar to a few months earlier, when I had bought my white poodle dress at The Leader Store and the following month, white high heels on sale at Crawford's Shoe Store for the same price each, as I had the nightgown of satin and silk.

She just might have a heart attack. But when I arrived home, she surprised me and actually hugged me and smiled when she ran her fingers through the nightgown. I think she may have murmured, at least it's practical and not a frilly see-through thing.

Don understood when I had explained why I couldn't stand at the altar in a white dress, before God. His comment was, "My good suit is powder blue. We'll look great together."

Jack and Pat agreed to stand up for us, and we agreed to do the same for them. I was conflicted about who to ask, my dad or my step-dad, to walk me down the aisle, and Pat was quiet about who could walk her. This led to the decision to have a double wedding.

No invitations were sent. The grooms presented their prospective brides with a wrist- sized cluster of miniature red roses, on top of a small white bible for us to carry.

I should have practiced walking in my dress with a hoop under it. However my attention was focused on how Don and Jack's heels were clicking together at the altar. I quickly realized you can't walk fast anywhere in new high heels, especially up the aisle on your wedding day, because the hooped ruffled dress started swaying forward and backward.

Even though Pat's calf-length white dress and my ankle-length blue dress was purchased before the decision was made to have a double wedding, we forever teased the guys that it became a double wedding, because neither wanted to pay the twenty-five dollar bet the two of them had had for years. Whoever got married first had to pay up.

Later, after the church basement reception, when I clamored in the front seat of Don's 1949 red Ford, *whoompf*—the bulk of my dress spread out over the dash of the car.

Wedding Day

"Recipe For Happiness"
Written for a niece's wedding shower

You have the ingredients for
   happiness. They begin
from this day forward when
   the two of you become one.

Trust your hearts and beliefs.
   Don't be afraid to ask for
advice, then take the time to
   review your decisions together.

Blend in your family circle
   which is strong because
they may have been where
   you are today.

Be patient when their
   love appears to
interfere with your
   precious time.

For life is so brief.
   Perfection so rare.
And laughter—
   with love is free.
God bless.

"The Pocket Mouse"

If I could be a pocket mouse—
   I would spend the whole day
with you, listening to your
   every thought—your problems
and happy times too.

I'd know what made you sad—
   and brought tears to your eyes,
or where I went wrong that day,
   and uncorked your anger
to my surprise.

Was it a flood that filled your day
   un-channeled little streams, or
just some un-reconcilable pebbles
   you've hid from me—to
spare me? Is that the key?

Yes. I know what makes you laugh
   and chuckle quietly.
So honey, just make believe I'm
   your pocket mouse and…
      Talk to me…
         Talk to me…
            Talk to me.

"Our First Visit to Virginia"

To visit Don's sister, Alice and family who had moved to a dairy farm. This wasn't the first time we had visited his family. But it was our first time to travel with our first-born, and it was the first time his parents had visited Virginia. I had the diaper pail at my feet, warmed his baby food on the dash, and didn't have to worry about his formula because I was breast-feeding.

I thank whoever told me about the new diaper safety pins that had a cap on the head of the pin that slid up and down, so there was no worry it would pop open and stick the baby.

Our vehicle didn't have seat belts for adults or safety seats for babies. I did have a canvas car bed that had a belt for the baby when lying down that could fit between his mom and dad.

The diaper bag was somewhere at my feet, as well. However, I had forgotten my sun-shade clippies that fastened over my glasses. I asked Don if he could stop in the next small town so I could buy new ones, which I might add, years later I left hanging in a peach tree in a pick-your-own orchard.

I entered this general store from the main street—but forgot I had made several turns inside this lovely store, and with package in hand rushed out the door. Whoa, I am lost! Where is our car? Where am I? Then I noticed, hilly or not, I recalled how Lima's Kresge's also was on a corner—of High and Main in 1956.

Now wouldn't you think I had learned my lesson when I rushed out to Lima's Macy's part of the mall to pick up a last minute wedding gift that the bride had requested and after calling all over town Macy's had one set left.

I rushed out the nearest exit and not only did the parking lot not look familiar, someone stole our new Grand Marques. I've got to find a phone and report it. However, when I rushed back inside, I questioned this isn't the men's department entrance. I was so embarrassed. The clerk just chuckled. I didn't have to say a word.

A special thank you to all the businesses who help those of us who still take a second when we park, to count the rows, etc. when we leave our vehicle in a parking lot or parking garage. Of course it always adds to the fun when I ask grand-children to help me remember.

Remembering when we had visited Thomas Jefferson's Monticello when the wood floors and furnishings sparkled like new, and then visiting it with grandchildren years later. Age had taken its toll, but the grandchildren were still just as interested in the clock he had designed, and the special wines that were sent up to the parlor from the wine cellar similar to how the food arrived to the dining room via a dumb-waiter from the kitchen which was located on the basement level.

We were disappointed to find that many of the civil war historical locations we had visited in the past had now been closed due to maintenance costs.

"The Dance"

My mom singing and
   groovin' to country songs
when she thought
   no one was listening.

One memorable night, I
   was baby-sitting my two
little sisters in the back-
   seat of our car while
it was parked outside
   a dance hall.

My sisters must have
   fallen asleep, because
only then would I have
   climbed out a window
and left them alone—
   but I didn't go far.

There must have been a
   full moon because it was
like daylight outside. The
   dance hall windows and
doors were open wide.

The music was familiar
  and when I peeked inside,
people were dancing in
  circles of eight. And, there
was my dad in his white shirt,
  trousers and shoes—on stage,
with a microphone, calling
  a square dance.

Some Sundays, his family would
  gather at his parent's farm house.
Three of my aunts, sang and played
  guitar. Dad may have called some
of these kitchen square dances.

Their toe-tapping music
  helped entertain the children
I had been delegated to keep
  contained in an adjoining room.

Before I finished the fourth grade,
  my parents had divorced. Years
later, my mom taught Dance at
  Arthur Murray Studio in Lima,
and her younger sister competed
  in Ballroom Dancing in Ft. Wayne.

Don taught me to dance, and I
 taught a grandson some of his
grandpa's moves at his wedding
 reception. I would still rather
dance, than run a marathon.

Early 1960's my dad and his 2nd wife
 accompanied Don and I and our
children on a visit to the Toledo Zoo.

Dad mentioned that the music drifting
 out of a nearby venue was one of
his favorite square dances, and asked
 me if I had ever danced to it. When
I said no, he gripped my waist and
 swung me around, to the rhythm
of "swing your partner" right there
 on the midway.

Later, however, his words to me
 alone, as we headed out to our
cars were, "Don't ever ask me to
 do this again."

This Sunday morning reminded me of Sundays spent with Don's family, which had been a regular gathering for years. Each family brought covered dishes to share at Don's one sister, Altha and her husband's country farm house in 1961.

Altha averaged four pies—and their mom, who was presently living in the back rooms of the farm-house averaged the same, filling the desert counter. However, there might be jello, cookies or puddings added by other attendees, as well.

While the ladies arranged the numerous dishes, the children could be outside playing, the men might be checking out someone's car or preparing the horse-shoe pitching area ready for pitching later.

After the meal, children were back outside and the ladies and men's card playing would soon be underway.

I was surprised when four little girls, ages 3 to 7 years old joined me as I closed both doors of their grandma's sitting room, so I would have privacy to breast-feed my seven-week old baby daughter. These girls were curious about a baby nursing without a bottle. Of course, I still threw a small blanket over my shoulder.

After the baby was satisfied and burped—these girls couldn't quit talking. That was so beautiful, they remarked. Then talked to the baby, gushing how beautiful her little fingers were—as smiles were shared and returned. Years later, as adults, they still talked about that afternoon.

I joined some of the family outside, with space to join Altha on her swing. A niece had picked a bright red King

David apple, polished it and bragged about finding one of the prettiest apples in the orchard that totaled forty-six trees, as she sat down on a lawn chair and joined us. Smiling, she took her first bite.

Suddenly, she held the apple out away from herself and screamed at the second half of a worm that was still wiggling in her apple. She turned away from us, spit the apple mess out of her mouth, shivered, and murmured "I've got to wash my mouth out."

We held our smiles and laughter until she left. I know I decided that day I would cut my apple in half before taking a bite.

When I first arrived in Lima, the day I graduated from high school, it was suggested that I attend the United Methodist Church because it was what I was used to. Besides, the minister was on the board at the children's home. My attendance was sporadic because when I wasn't attending class, I was working a few hours after school, plus working a full day on Saturday and Sunday.

Years later, the minister who had baptized four of my children didn't appear to mind that I brought my children there for Sunday School and always waited for them at the back of the church, close to the exit, so I didn't disturb other adult Sunday School Classes.

As soon as my children came up the stairs with other children who were being collected by their parents, we left. We had our Ford station wagon at the time.

This particular Sunday, a man approached me and it took me a moment to recall where I had met him. Then it dawned on me when he mentioned his wife's name. They had sat at an adjoining table at our high-school alumni. His wife had graduated a year behind me in school. He said, "My wife's birthday is next week and I'm driving myself crazy deciding what to get her. Any ideas?"

"Do you usually give her something she needs or something for the house?" I replied. The blush on his face was the only answer I needed. "Had you thought of the two of you going to a dinner-theatre and overnight in a hotel out of town?"

He smiled and said, "I want it to be a surprise, too."

He left towards another part of the church and I turned around to wait for my children, when I noticed a group of about five women and the minister in a conversation down in the front of the empty church.

I didn't pay too much attention to them until the minister approached me and said, "I think it best if you not return to this church." I was stunned. Then he briskly walked away, and disappeared down the same hall the young man had taken. I looked at my calendar, its 1967.

When I turned around to wait for my children, my eyes had been drawn down towards the women and they had all turned their backs. I had been judged. Why? No guts. No eye contact from him or those women. What was their problem? I had dropped off papers to his wife at the minister's home at some point in time. It wasn't like I was a stranger.

Numerous children were gathering to meet their parents and mine quickly joined me.

I was crushed. Broken-heartened that an educated man—a minister no less, had listened to a group of straight-laced bidies who had judged me because of their filthy minds regarding a two-minute conversation with the spouse of a high-school friend.

Now. The rest of the story. Years later—I received a phone call from this young man. He had just buried his wife. I hadn't noticed it in the paper because I wasn't familiar with her married name.

"Can we talk?"

I replied, "Sure." I could hear the raw pain in his voice. "My wife." He talked and talked about their life—her illness—about his business—about the weather. I just listened. Perhaps a brief comment now and then. After about an hour, his voice softened, he stammered a bit, and said, "Thank you for listening."

I never heard from him again.

"Time Marches On"

Time Marches On as
   the Clock keeps ticking:
A moment…
   A blink of the eye…
A beat of the heart…
   A conversation…
A sunrise…A sunset…

The newborns
   demands
appease hunger.
   With awareness
their limited
   world expands.

Observance, understanding,
   desires fulfilled. Failure
doesn't exist. Fall down. Get
   up. But accepts the box.

Then questions, are all the stars
   too far away to reach, to touch?
If friends can do it, why not I?
   Oh, the box has windows, doors
where time is clocked.

Creative responsibility fills one's
   pockets. Values change. When
did that happen? Time just kept a beat:
   Tick-Tock, Tick-Tock, Tick-Tock.

Through love and joy, the touching
   of another soul, the miracle of new
life. Mixed blessings and growth comes
   full circle.

Time is measured. Constant, yet
   changing. And the Lord was there.
Not a shadow—but an essence.

Don was bowling an extra makeup game in time to qualify for the 1969 season tournaments, and wasn't home yet when the phone rang. I was pregnant at the time and it took me a bit to answer the phone.

I answered and whoever called talked about Don like they knew him well. I recalled one of the bowlers on his team had called me earlier in the season and had asked me to accompany Don to the bowling alley, just once. Because there is a young woman who has been hanging around Don and that more than one bowler had told her he was married, had a lovely wife and children.

But I hadn't followed their advice. I knew my insecurities were tangling like I had swallowed a vitamin pill without fluid. Don had told me about a woman on his bread route who answered her door in a sheer nighty and he acted a bit embarrassed to even talk about it. Although, during the time he had this route, he had doubled his customers. Then someone who had seniority over him took over his route and he was assigned a different one. At least where he worked now his job didn't work like that.

All of this was ringing in my heart and I finally asked, "Did you say you wanted me to give him a message?" There was a heart-breaking silence when I heard two young female voices giggle before they hung up. Wow! I never found out who it was but I sat there holding the phone as I had stretched the cord as far as it would go.

Why would someone make a phone call like that? Their idea of fun? I questioned how many of these calls had they made? You know, Lord, I thought, so am I really that gullible? I trust Don. As usual, he expects me to fight my own battles. Although, once in a while it would be nice if he would step in the middle for me. However, he would probably just laugh about this.

Then, I was reminded of an evening when we had joined Don's niece and nephew to stop at a country music dance-hall after a steak dinner out of town. Even Russel, who still limped with a metal brace from polio, had sent a young woman practically tripping over her own feet to get away from him, after she had just brazenly plopped herself on his lap—uninvited.

Don and Russ's Nola were still on the dance floor. I moved around the table—sat beside him and teasingly asked, "What in the world did you do?"

"I told her, "You see that red head out there? She's my wife and she's hades-on-wheels when anyone messes with her man! I'd move now if I were you!"

Divorced and a single mom, our mom had finally found a good, steady job and someone she trusted, who agreed to take care of her three daughters. Her ex-husband had still to pay any child support.

Which is how we came to live with the family of one our mom's distant cousins who offered to take us in. She and her family had a spare room in their huge farmhouse in the country.

As mom struggled to make ends meet, she had a room to rent, but no car because the bulk of her paycheck must have gone for our care.

I was in the fifth grade, but had always had the responsibility of taking care of my little sisters for as long as I could remember, and was used to helping with dishes and laundry. However, once in a while a memory kicked me off my lazy duff—'pay-for-your-keep'; and I helped feed the chickens but vowed I would never raise chickens after shoveling out the brooder-house filled with baby chicks.

A year later, mom had to find us another place to live and I asked Mrs. Nancy what I could do to thank her for taking care of the three of us all this time. Her reply was, "Just pass it on."

Many years later, her comment came to mind when a neighbor and his wife stopped by and asked me if I would consider babysitting their friend and business partner's five children. He had been granted custody and couldn't find anyone who was willing to be a live-in nanny.

His five children were similar in age to mine; his youngest was in diapers and so was mine. Without my knowledge, they had already acquired a judge's approval for me to have legal custody of his children while he was at work.

As I considered their request, I had no idea that this was something that had lingered in my thoughts all these years. And I never really understood how much our mom had struggled to find the right solution for us.

Thus, my husband came home from work to find our brood had doubled in size and he never once complained. This set-up lasted a bit over one year. Eight children rode the school bus to and from my house—sometimes this included breakfast. One cookie sheet of cookies were gone before they had a chance to cool.

My previous five-year's experience as one of two cook's helpers, preparing meals to serve eighty in the children's home kitchen certainly came in handy. I don't recall any time when any of these ten children were ever sick that year.

His eight year old was mocked at school when he referred to me as his mom. In tears, he said "Well, she is my substitute mom." My husband and I took all ten to Findlay for a summer outing and we stopped at a dairy for ice cream on our way home. The owner came up to me and said, "Oh, honey, they aren't all yours are they?" Some were blondes—some were brunettes and I replied, "No. Half of them are mine and half are not." His oldest daughter smiled and took her baby brother by the hand to help him with his upside-down cone with a smiley face.

This stint ended when their dad remarried and his bride retired from teaching school to become their full-time mom.

"Fences and Gossip"

There's an old Cowboy Country
   Western song, 'Don't Fence Me
In'. As the I don't like fences melody
   rang around in my thoughts—

a true reminder of how many
   times, I have felt stuck—literally
sitting-on-the-fence of indecision.
   Yes. No. Maybe. Are you certain?

What was he thinking, I wondered
   when a family member shoved my
entrance door so hard, he nearly
   knocked the Dad of the children

I was babysitting off his feet, as
   he was standing on my entry door
rug—waiting while I was across the
   room fastening his two-year-child's

snowsuit. His others had their coats
   on, ready to go home with their
Dad. I asked the intruder, "Do you
   need something?" His face was

flushed, and he stammered, "Can I
   borrow your jumper cables?"
"Don has them in his car. He'll be home
in a little bit, if you need to wait."

No one ever asked me why I had agreed
   to accept the responsibility of taking
care of someone else's children,
   so their Dad could work.

You see, Home has changed many times
   in my lifetime. But I'm not the child I
once was—like when my dad and his
   mother insisted my sisters and I had

to move. I asked the lady, "How can I
   thank you for welcoming us into your
home, so our Mom could work and
   not have to worry about our care?"
She replied, "Someday, just pass it on."

Perhaps some still see me as an outsider.
   I didn't go to school around here,
so what was my neighbor in such a tizzy
   about? What was he expecting to see?

Two days later, we were at a family dinner,
   and there were several women in the
kitchen doing dishes. Nola was washing,
   and the rest of us were drying or storing.

"Hey, Marilyn! Tell me how you can get
it on with two men—with ten kids in the
   house…when I can't seem to get
lucky with one kid in the house."

Complete silence twisted my insides. Shock!
 Was this a joke? But no one was laughing.
The impossibility of such a travesty was
 common sense! But they believed it.

They walked away. Nothing I could have said
 would have mattered. A dear friend once
told me, you and Don know the truth. That's
 all that matters. But, I knew Don would
probably just laugh and say, "Ignore them."
 And…I thought I had.

But how does one not question such nonsense?
 I've seen and felt what happens to the
children when marriages are torn apart,
 when lies are spread. Some joyfully

repeated until others also believe their
 treachery, totally forgetting a family of
children separated from their mom,
 struggling, attending school, riding a

different school-bus, and later going home
 each evening to an empty house with their
Dad, after I, their nanny/baby-sitter,
 had greeted them with a smile, all of us

doing the best we could. However,
 gossip can melt the icing off a cake,
when those who repeatedly whispered,
 had set off some bubbling fireworks.

Our marriage was as rock-solid
   as most, but what if it hadn't been?
Let's not forget our five children as well.
   Gossip is a slippery slope of lies.

And. I still don't have a moment to waste
   on speculation. Just leave behind this
thought. What goes around, comes around.
   I pray it doesn't ever happen to anyone.

"Smile And Pass It On"

A smile is a mile-marker-smile
   but only when it's returned, for
then it stretches for miles and miles.

Children don't question or hesitate,
   but beam its return, sparking
instantaneous, reflecting lasers—
   into a kaleidoscope of hope.

But to those who answer with a
   turned-down frown, questioning
why we smiled at them—then just
   shrug and shuffle off in a fog.

Wouldn't you like to say,
   hey, it takes less effort to
smile than frown, don't you see?
We're happy to be alive Today!

So, Smile. Smile. Smile.
   Light up your corner of the world
and hope the doubters wonder why.
   Why we rejoice in life's song,
and smile,
   and pass it on.

While at Trails End Lodge on Pigeon Lake, Ontario, Canada—the flags of Canada and the U.S.A. gently waved in a cool morning breeze.

A light fog hovered over the lake. Dew lay heavy on the lawn. Tiny insects floated in the morning sunlight like weightless mustard seeds.

Four men smoothly motored out in the Bass Boat they had towed from home, just at sunrise. The water was as still as wavy glass. They took their packed lunch and were not expected back until mid-afternoon, unless the fishing was exceptional.

With notebook in hand I joined a couple who were occupied reading books. Looking out at the horizon in the direction the fishermen had disappeared, I noticed the picture I had been told would surprise me. The boring Rockpile was off-shore of the Island and the approach to Trails End Lodge. Seagulls were perched on the Rockpile, so still—they appeared to be fishermen in a boat.

Closer to shore, I watched a mother mallard duck skim by the shoreline—chattering to her eight little ducklings following her at a seemingly effortless pace. Then, it appeared she played our human peek-a-boo with them.

She hopped up on the square raft just a few yards off-shore. Her brood huddled close to the raft as she continued to chatter to them. By the time they were two-thirds of the way around, she hopped off the raft—counting them before they continued on their journey, dutifully following behind her.

Suddenly we heard the Bass Boat moving in at a pretty good clip and it wasn't noon yet.

They had returned because the wind had picked up—causing white caps, which meant it was too dangerous to be out. After they secured the boat inside the boat shelter, they cleaned their catch and we went in to Bobcageon for some shopping and groceries. Then we stopped at the Kawartha Dairy for ice cream cones.

When we returned to Trails End Lodge, we noticed off in the distance across the lake, the sky looked troubled. As it approached, I noticed—as did others—how Pigeon Lake reflected the color of the sky as the swirling water quickly turned from indigo blue to charcoal gray, to scary midnight black.

We couldn't see the sun or the moon. It was hard to distinguish the skyline from the water as the wind battled to the depths of Pigeon Lake. Swales of water and the sky became a misty pale gray. The Bass Boat's movement that morning had left continuous wrinkled ripples on the lake's surface. However, this storm was splashing water against the concrete wall that framed the beautiful lawn apart from the lake, with the power of a cascading waterfall.

It appeared the storm was infuriated as the wind thundered water against the concrete wall shoreline—that had the audacity not to move out of the way. We ate our evening meal while the wind continued to hang around.

The storm finally passed. The wind subsided. Soon the surface of Pigeon Lake calmed like drifting sand and near the island was the comforting distinct song of a Great Northern Loon and an echo of its mate?

A welcome sweet sunset mirrored the smooth-as-glass blue water while patches of powder blue sky peeked between lazy clouds of gray which lingered in the distance.

Reminiscent of life—when and how others' expectations affect and sometimes rebound with those we love.

"The Swamp"

Rice grass, lily pads and seaweed sway
   merely skimming the surface midst
      fallen logs from winters past—abandoned
         dangerous deterrents, to speeding motor boats.

The setting sun cast eerie shadows, while
   silent, sweeping oars are dipped gracefully
      into still blue green water, stirring
         Muskie and Large-Mouth Bass
            challenging them to play
               with the fisherman's spoon.

Dusk triggered a surrounding chorus of bullfrogs,
   the unmistakable laughter of the Great Northern Loon,
      the guttural croon of a shadowed Blue Heron
         just past time of the mosquito on the
            inlet swamp of Canada's Pigeon Lake.

Prompt:
Describe how phone service has changed from the past

The neighborhood party line has become…texting messages to an unlimited number of family, friends or business associates. Not the warm sound of their voice.

A visit, a letter, a walk or a drive might once have been cheaper. And writing a letter doesn't result in instantaneous replies. Try typing with carbon paper. No errors?

Guess again. No delete or backspace here! Long fancy nails? Not possible, but definitely a challenge. The availability of paper? Paper was scarce. As were books. Thus libraries were born.

During World War II: Rationing affected the general population: one pair of shoes a year. Sometimes the children went barefoot until time for school to start. Adults found ways to make their shoes last longer, too, like having new soles stitched on, worn heels replaced. Cardboard to cover the worn-through soles, and hand-me-down shoes were still better than none.

However, it is still possible to have favorite shoes, boots, and purses repaired/renewed.

Properly darned socks could be just as soft and sometimes a bit more-roomy. New fabric was expensive. My grandmother made three-year-old me a winter coat from the best part of her previous winters' coat. Then, I did the same for one of my daughters. A dress made out of a porch sale, twenty-five cent new curtain, that didn't fit any windows, anyhow. Padded animal knee patches from clothes worn thin or outgrown.

Patchwork quilts made from scraps of new and gently worn garments continues today as an art. A designer's dream with warmth. Or join a quilters group—who become friends and quilts become cherished family heirlooms.

However, where some things have made life easier, and faster, does it appear that some-times creativity has been stolen from some, whereas solemn appreciation has grown for others.

Give some children today a lump of clay, even play dough, and they see it as a lump? Yesterday's child would see possibilities shaped into a bird. A dog. A dipper. A cup or spoon.

Paper and pencil to sketch an image, write a story, or a poem. A knife in a wood carver's hand.

What's a time piece? One you have to wind. Wristwatch? Today's phone offers not only the time, but more advantages and information availability than one could ever have dreamt of.

Today's phone is not only a phone, but a time piece, a camera, a dictionary, the news, weatherreports, stock market, email, address for connected groups, and more techie reports than I care to read in a day's time.

My sisters enjoyed the sounds of their coo-coo-clocks. Some Swiss-carved miniatures twirling the musical hour.

Fallen leaves end up in the compost instead of the scent of burning leaves. Then, line-dried clothes in a summer breeze have a fresh-air scent, unless a new neighbor has yet to learn not to burn her trash on Monday mornings, which today's clothes-dryers have also changed.

The scent and feel of a newborn in my arms and singing soothing, silly songs to them. Including the creaking sound and comfort of rocking a child and self in quiet contemplation.

The hum of a sewing machine with the satisfaction of a properly fitted garment. Searching the button box for matching buttons. Replacing a zipper, by hand or machine. Detailed hand stitches. Embroidery to frame. Ironing. Pressing. The scent of steaming starch.

What hasn't changed is the perception of age, friends and family. When I was much younger, I was so busy just keeping my children fed, clothed and support to whatever they were interested in such as, sports, music, school projects, etc. But there was still time to proudly appreciate and watch them grow, change, and glory in their smiles—to know the joy of being blessed with the opportunity to be a stay-at-home mom, and observe their personalities emerge. To just be there, when they needed a bump soothed, a tear dried, struggles encouraged and quietly allow my pride in them to shine.

Aging was so far in the future, but dying young was still a crushing blow. When my Mom was unexpectedly put on a gurney by the rescue squad, I kissed her on the cheek for the first time as an adult. A few months later I said goodbye, for forever, this time.

It was like a part of me had just disappeared and left behind memories that brush through my thoughts. Photos help, but her voice is but a gentle nudge. Her laughter, like a breeze that came from next door and brought with it a memory. Once taken so for granted. Humming her favorite song, yet thoughts seldom shared or understood—forever lost, if we don't take the time to share whenever possible.

P.S. During a phone conversation with one of my daughters who was babysitting her granddaughter—I listened—as my daughter said to her granddaughter, "You made the mess—you clean it up." Followed by the great-granddaughter doing as she was told, in a sing/song voice repeated three times or more, "You made the mess—you clean it up." One adult teaching the big/little lessons of life. That's love.

"Release…The Butterfly"

Imprisoned in a vacuum,
   Alone. Unaware.
Silent. Untouched.

Feeling no pain, no fear
   no compassion, no love,
encapsulated in a fog.

Sealed in a universe of darkness
   the detached memory of
a careless cocoon.

Soon…soon…soon…
   springtime brings understanding
and releases the fragile butterfly
   to fly free—venture off in any direction.

In the early days my parents were always looking for ways to earn extra money. From Dad trapping for skins to sell, and raising a few turkeys to sell for the holidays, to caring for a road-side rest that came with a house, grassy area to keep mowed and two out-houses for public use, one for men and one for women. It also included a gas-station, that during World War II, it meant all-service, which Mom handled while my Dad was on the road, driving truck.

While he was married to Mom, he didn't spend much time at home with us. Odd that I don't recall a whole lot then, perhaps because I was too busy taking care of my little sisters, and helping Mom in the Pastime Park business.

After their tumultuous divorce, he married one of the women he had been running with, pretty much most of the years of his marriage with Mom.

He lived within twenty miles from the children's home where my sisters and I grew up. I started the 7th grade through graduation. Dad visited about a half dozen times all the six years I was there.

Even less after we married. He was a trucker and stopped by my house when Don and I lived in Beaverdam to see his first grandchild. But he never stopped or visited again unless she was along.

Many years later he was in the hospital. His wife wasn't there at the time and he and I actually talked and listened to each other. He didn't make any demands or promises, but had a few excuses: "You were strong, smart, brave, you didn't need me." He also told me he loved me. As I started to leave, he kissed me on the cheek, and I kissed him on the cheek, goodbye. This was our final goodbye.

However, there is one saying that really ticks me off. "The acorn doesn't fall from the tree." It is from the bible somewhere. I am not responsible for my dad's lifestyle and choices over his lifetime. I choose to refuse to be that acorn!

Note: Mom visited the children's home every chance she was allowed. Once a month, the second Sunday of the month, from 2:00-4:00pm. She took the Greyhound Bus to Bellevue, a Taxi from Bellevue to the children's home. The Taxi picked her up for her return trip. After she married my step-dad, George, he drove her many times.

Marilyn & her dad

"Marking Time"

As seasons mark time
   leaping from spring
to fall,

the winters of life
   speed into
overdrive,

bursting with life
   new and
renewed,

like a colony of
   ladybugs welcoming
another spring.

"The Soul and the Spirit"

Research regarding the
   soul and the spirit
revealed that sometimes
   the two also appear
as partners.

But does the soul,
   master guardian of
the mind and heart
   reside in the
breath of Life?

Understandable, for
   the first breath of a
new born is granted a
   unique combination of
soul, spirit and DNA.

And when one draws their
   last breath exhales
their soul and spirit as
   gently as a whisper
or the roar of a lion.

This dependable Soul
   may consist of compassion
forged in courageous tenacity,
   and a heart forecasting a
gracious destiny.

The mystery of our alike/
 differences joins with
the harmony of a forgiven
 soul, and perhaps with
the expectation of

immortality—trusting they
 will someday join
yesterdays angels as their
 prayers strengthen the
spirit of the Lord within.

The inspiration of
 one's spirit creates
memories of a
 sparkling smile,
unforgettable

personality, and the
 distinctive sound of
one's voice, combined—
 equals the magic of hearts
in tune with the universe.

Before writing my novel *The Flutist and the Dancer*, most of the articles I found during my research regarding children's homes, were negative. Many focused on the costs, the dollars and cents, and not the results of children raised in a children's home.

In 1986, I interviewed a Special Children's Services Supervisor who represented the changes in how they handled choices for placing children, after they were taken from their parents. Their initial goal was to reunite children with their parents. In the meantime, the children were placed elsewhere while the parents underwent counseling.

In the nineties, children were placed in the children's home as a temporary holding place, or placed in foster care. A caseworker has to prove what the parents were guilty of to have their children taken away from them.

I knew first-hand of a family who had fostered numerous children for over twenty years. Some of the children were with them for a few weeks, others stayed on longer.

Interviews with these almost adult children – revealed, the children were angry because they were taken away from their parents—no matter the circumstances. They could be resentful, despondent and fight accepting the foster parents.

The hardest part of this new temporary foster care was when the siblings were separated, as well. At times, the children might be returned to the parents, only to once again be returned to the children's home.

Some churches worked with children that were on this back and forth, upside down living arrangement. All the while, especially when parents weren't married, generation after generation continued this cycle. There is a passage in the Bible that preaches children are likened to the Acorn not falling far from the parental tree.

In all the six years I was at the Flat Rock Children's Home, with daily morning worship, plus church on Sunday morning and evening, and prayer meeting on Wednesday night, not once did I ever hear such a message.

I was married with children when a minister focused the Father's Day Sunday morning worship on this very statement. 'No way,' I thought. I was so angry that I wrote my feelings down on my church bulletin. 'Don't Assume!' I thought only of myself at that point, and wrote, NO. NO. NO.

How discouraging for children of a father who was a flagrant skirt-chaser. I watched how sad my mom was when she waited for him. This was not the type of person I wanted to marry or see my children deal with, or copy. I prayed, and the Lord helped me make my decision after I met my husband and his family before we were married.

At our last Flat Rock Children's Home Reunion, someone would jokingly ask, "Did you ever have trouble finding a job?"

No way. We had learned, through training, how to work and have pride in the results, whether it was plowing a straight furrow in the field, collecting potatoes by the bucketful in the field, ironing the Big Boys Sunday Shirts, setting a proper table in the dining room, doing the dishes, milking cows, washing windows, or gathering eggs.

But I had a head start on the other children, because from the day my mom taught me how to make change, my dad might stop by with a basket of melons for instance and said to me, "sit under that tree and don't come in until they are sold". Mom would have been the one to help me make a sign posting the price. Weekends were best.

"The Patchwork Quilt"

We went home again
   but just for a visit,

an extension
   of childhood memories.

We turned the page of
   time and found

we're still brothers,
   sisters, friends.

The shared frustrations,
   loneliness, acceptance
and laughter, binds us
   together like a
     patchwork quilt.

The topping; each colorful
   personality, unique.
The batting; our loving
   trust in God, and
     each other.
The backing, family and
   the Children's Home.

A children's home sister and I had updated addresses and phone numbers for a previous Children's Home Reunion, and had scheduled a meeting to tie-up a few things.

I really wasn't certain if I would be staying the night, but packed something just in case the meeting ran late. We had decided on a time, so I had planned to arrive a few minutes early.

When I opened the door to the restaurant, the scent of fresh-baked cinnamon rolls was a welcoming memory. As my eyes adjusted from the bright sunlight to the shadowed interior. I greeted, "Hi everybody."

Not so memorable was that no one replied. Their empty plates, and their silence was surprisingly rude. Plus all five of them were studying several pages of whatever. It was apparent, the meeting had started without me. So I finally asked politely, "Lauri, did you find out about the music for the sing-along we discussed?"

Finally, she replied, "Well, you might remember Helen, but since you live out of town and all. Helen knows about putting together reunions, and she isn't interested in the sing-along."

"I see," I replied as I glanced at the names and assignments they had listed on a brochure laying on the table. My name wasn't listed anywhere. "You invited me to this meeting today for nothing? I drove over an hour for nothing? I see you don't have anyone listed for publicity."

Helen quickly responded, "If you are referring to the

Bellevue Gazette, I will take care of that."

"Fine," I replied. Although the scent of those cinnamon rolls made my stomach growl, I was certain food was not on the menu for me right now. "Since you have everything under control, I'll be heading home then."

Suddenly, Debbie jumped up with tears in her eyes. "I can't believe you're treating her like this. She's always been helpful in the past. Sent out invitations after searching for address changes and all that."

"I've got her old list," Helen smiled.

When I turned to leave, Debbie rushed to my side and hugged me. "This wasn't fair to you," she murmured as she walked me to my car and added, "Call me if you need me for anything."

I nodded. Carelessly stuffing their brochure in my briefcase, I swallowed back angry tears—especially after what I had overheard before the door closed—"Oh, she'll be fine. Nothing ever bothers her."

Perhaps once in a-while I should say what I'm thinking. I've heard the squeaky wheel gets things done. Well, it at least makes a lot of noise.

I was stunned with the way the trip had turned out. Then I recalled this Helen person had asked me who had put me in charge, a few years back at a previous gathering. At the time, I was so busy checking people off an arrival list, I let it slide, but was tempted to reply, 'No one. I asked and was met with approval.' I've heard some say, you can't go home again, but this was a first for me.

I stopped on the way home for a coffee-to-go, and it dawned on me, they hadn't even left room or a chair for me at their table. When I arrived home, I read through an article about the Flat Rock Children's Home in the Sandusky Register I had saved.

I called and asked if they would be interested in writing a story about former residents of the Flat Rock Children's Home—gathering for a Reunion. He replied, "One of our writers, Sheila will be in touch."

I gave Sheila, the journalist, the committee's plans, and she was excited.

Then I received a message that Helen had backed out of organizing the reunion because her husband was ill, and wondered if I could help.

The day arrived.

I understand some thought Sheila and I were old friends. She and I were early, and she asked me questions about the different buildings and why today was so important to me. Then somewhere in the background I heard someone using their in-charge voice, announce that it was time for the Tour of the Girls Cottage.

However, no one was listening to Helen. I supposed it was because of a few late arrivals. Squeals and laughter and hugs abounded.

Helen approached me with her clipboard highlighted Flat Rock Reunion 1987, and asked, "Will you please announce that it is time for the Tour of the Girls' Cottage?"

There were about thirty people standing in the huge parking area where most of us had parked and I waited for the newest arrival noise to calm down, and turned around and said, "Hey guys, we're headed for the Girls' Cottage."

I looked for Sheila. She nodded. There was no need

to announce anything else. Quiet conversations would be the norm. Sheila quickly joined us, taking notes, even though she had asked our permission to run her recorder.

Of course, the guys made comments of never having been in certain sections of the Girls' Cottage. There had been some changes. After a few chuckles followed, a lady twice my age commented, "They never locked the Little Girls sitting room door. I wonder how many years, our boy-friends were sneaking in to see us." That one was a surprise to me. I had never seen the door open.

The day, meals, visiting, hugs and an unusually quiet Helen appeared to go well.

A week or so later, Sheila sent me copies of the front page, plus one inside page that were impressive. She reported comments and greeting responses, and stories shared.

I received a phone call from Debbie. "Helen is fit to be tied. The Bellevue paper printed their usual announcement. She was royally upset because her name isn't mentioned once. On top of that, not only was your picture in the paper, but also one of your sister."

Spending a few hours with Sheila that day was like spending time with a friend. Her interesting questions meant she cared about each person she interviewed. I had unknowingly picked up her mannerisms and style which was apparent when I started interviewing and writing articles for 'The Senior's Beacon' monthly news. I was also working on my family history, Don's family history annual news and my first novel.

I felt she wanted to be there that day. Every question she asked, and our responses appeared in print in the newspaper. She had an inquiring mind that was contagious. Others were drawn to her personality, her smile. Her focus for the descriptive reunion became more interesting because she caught the excitement, the joy and the pride which was also revealed in the photos.

My angry frustration melted because I had followed-up on a hunch to call the Sandusky Register, which became a blessing in disguise. I had found my writing niche.

"The Reunion"
World of Poetry 11-21-1987—Golden Poet Award 1988

Arrivals cluster like
  birds gathering to
    fly south.
Old-new faces greet and nod as
  hello-handshakes ignite
    recognition.

Then surprise unlocks
  unanticipated feelings.
Emotions erupt,
  are outrageously renewed,
    and joyously relived.

Shedding a feather of pretense,
  they become children,
unfettered by titles and roles,
  unafraid to ask
    unanswered questions.

For today, it's okay
  to drop the mask—
    appreciate their differences.

Then all too soon—time intervenes,
  draws near the poignant,
imminent parting of this children's-
  home-family's, loving promises and
    cherished memories.

Reluctance sparkles as the huddles
   dissipate and merge into
     mere sunset silhouettes
        in the rear view mirror.

"Finding My Way in the Field of Writing"

I've found the quickest way to find out what a story needs is: research. Okay, I've heard and read numerous articles in writer magazines. I've studied the book titled, *Goal, Motivation & Conflict—The Building Blocks of Good Fiction* by Debra Dixon. Gryphon Books for Writers, Memphis, Tennessee.

In fact, I mentioned this book to my editor at Denlinger's Publishers that I follow these guidelines religiously. This got her attention. However, Denlinger's had already accepted my first novel, *The Flutist and the Dancer,* before I purchased *Goal, Motivation & Conflict.*

I have a fat folder of over 50 query letters which included a SASE, (self-addressed stamped envelope enclosed) which were rejection replies. A couple of them took the time to correspond with encouraging words.

I also entered short story contests for magazines, and sometimes questioned if the entry or query was ever read.

Some found numerous things wrong. Others sent replies, such as: Not interested. Timing was wrong. The story was missing notable details. My ideas were very good—but the reader gets lost at times. But don't give up. Your writing has promise. Give the reader a reason to turn the pages. Your research speaks volumes. Are you certain this isn't autobiographical? You're doing better at not leaving any loose ends—no questions left unanswered.

However, I continued to search through magazines I

borrowed from the Lima Public Library and read books from the library as well. I bought books by certain authors to learn how they handled their characters and locations, for instance. Choices are astronomical. I found I enjoyed research. If my character was going to need information—for just a moment—the more research I collected notes on, the easier it was to allow my character and me to be acquainted with a specific situation.

I attended workshops, and learned even more when our Lima Area Writer's Club directed several writer's workshops. Because, when we sponsored a workshop for aspiring writers, I had to do in-depth research—so I could answer questions others might need answers to.

Stream of consciousness

can be a who knows—after years and years—how one heart tuned-in to another Who knows when the snow melts off the mountain who camped there in the fall—who knows as the river flowed by—what rocks—What trees—What mountains it passed by—who traversed its water way in search of food—search of a new life—in search of a spouse—a friend—

Who knows its true ancestry when the wanderer never returned—but just continued on—with one more mountain to climb—one more prairie to hunt through—one more cool wooded area to meander—one more sunrise—one more sunset- that of the migratory, the Indian—

The explorer now—their inquiring minds—takes them into space—beyond the ocean's surface—and into the science lab—sorting—dividing molecules—and delving into mysteries of the mind—where do these thoughts originate from—Do they sift through the element of time— are they beamed-in from the past or the future --

Visions of imaginary—dreams of the impossible—questing—ringing—almost, but not quite touching—passing through the blankets of disbelief—presenting puzzles of the truth of life—but the puzzles seem to be guided by magnetic poles—moving in another direction just when it seems they fit like a glove—

That's when the picture becomes blurry and nonsensical—when we again wonder why we do what we do—and why as time marches to yet another beat—another march—another life—as death ceases the heartbeat on earth—it breathes life into the yet unborn—

Thoughts—words—feelings—have always drifted through my mind—day-dreaming my Latin teacher called it—her voice always seems to inspire me—but not in the direction she intended—so now this morning 47 plus years later—the birds are still singing—the grass is still green—the maple trees sway in the cool morning September breeze—the corn field will soon be harvested—my children are all grown and will soon be living on their own.

July 30, 1951

Forever destined to always be standing on the outside looking in? I was fifteen and walking from the Flat Rock Post Office back to the Flat Rock Children's Home Big Girls Cottage with a friend, when dusk settled earlier than expected.

The houses were about five feet from the sidewalk. We really weren't window peeping—not in a sadistic way but in a wistful, missing, wishing-way, for something we no longer had. A home.

The house didn't have to be a mansion to qualify. In fact, it was usually the moderately priced homes.

Dusk. The time of day when the moon and the sun played hide and seek. When lights inside a house magically, gradually are turned on. For the observer, lights revealed family photos on walls that reflected warmth and trophies through open windows. Someone was playing the piano. Lace transparent curtains revealed mere silhouettes of the family. We heard children's laughter, and a baby crying, as a friend and I slowly walked by.

June 30, 1991

Now I had all this—yet here I stood, in my own backyard. Fireflies winking their mysterious flight. The warm amber glow of a lamp near the window was a comforting sight.

A grapevine wreath framed an embroidered barn scene. Voices of my family, blended in competition with the television. A plant and figurine in the kitchen window above the sink, brought to mind reminders of a someday home that hovered in my memory.

Tears surprised me as the scent of cigarette smoke replaced the scent of cherry scented pipe smoke. It had all come full circle—from the memorable evening at dusk to my today home, not a stranger's.

My picture of home is where I come to, when the rest of the world is too busy to see the real me. Home. Where I can go barefoot—barefaced to hide my real self is unnecessary because it is here where there is unqualified love.

These expectations are mine alone. Here where I can be silly—angry—explosive—loving, tearfully be myself. No apologies. No need.

But yet, there were still times when I felt I was on the outside looking into my husband's heart, even after almost forty years, he still kept a piece of himself in reserve. He could show more gusto and excitement about getting to the golf course than being with me, and get so involved in a football game on television, that he actually ate beef liver saturated with French's Worcestershire Sauce, and he hates beef liver.

Hey, I tried golf but there was no competition. Playing golf with me as his partner was about as boring as waiting for a flower to bloom. But on vacations that we did together, or with those who we were traveling with. It was pretty awesome. Include dancing in this category. He was much better than me, but that didn't matter because when he boogied-down—jitter-bugging with me, it really didn't matter because he was looking at me.

So, my feelings of insecurity are, perhaps, because I set my expectations beyond common sense, and turned to writing. He once told me he didn't know me until I started writing.

"Writing Challenges"

In the beginning,
   writing became
a way to calm my
   frustrations

on rainy and snowy
   weekends when as
a teen, I couldn't
   possibly ride my
1949 thru early 1953

bicycle to no-where.
   From the archway
at the Children's Home
   Girls Cottage—

towards the Main
   Building kitchen drive,
then the grade school
   sidewalk,

cruise to the stone
   drive and past the
laundry building,
   the boiler house,

and around again as
   fast as I could pedal,
three to five times,
   then slowed to relax—

Enjoying the sound of
   the tires—allowing
time for angry tears to
   dry. I never gave it

a thought that no
   one ever stopped
me, and I never
   once wiped out.

Writing letters to my
   mom was usually
relaxing, but not that
   day. I couldn't chance

that the office might
   read it. Mrs. A called
all us girls and matron
   to the study room.

Then called me to join
   her to the front of the
Study Table, and again
   asked why I stole a

small, rusty tin of a
   spice I had never heard
of before. I repeated my
   reply to that question

just as I had in the
   kitchen when she had
grabbed it out of my
   hand, that Matron had

asked me to borrow it
   for her. "Now admit
that you lied," she
   demanded. I shook

my head no. She turned
   me around and said,
"Bend over," and flipped
   up my dress, and whacked

me with the paddle she had
   brought with her. Matron
stood there (I could see
   her shoes) and watched

while I took a whipping,
   knowing she wasn't
allowed to cook on her
   hot-plate in her room.

I never cried, and I lost
   track of how many
times she whacked me.
   But, she suddenly

stopped and the room
   was quiet except for
her high-heels clomping
   out and down the stairs.

I straightened, and pulled
   my dress down and in
place. My hands ached
   where I had gripped

the chair. I didn't want
   to see anyone, but the
room was empty. With
   her demands still

ringing in my ears, I
   hid behind the open
door and the wall, still
   trying to figure out

why. Nothing made any
   sense. What lesson was
she hoping to resolve? I
   didn't have any use for

this stupid spice, and she
   knew it. Well, riding
my bicycle was out of
   the question. But, one

thing for certain, I would
   have to steer clear of
both of these women for
   ten months, until I

graduated from high
   school. I used paper
I wasn't supposed to use,
   wrote, then tore it up

and flushed the pieces
   down the toilet. But,
the humiliation wasn't
   that easy to get rid of.

Even though no one spoke
   of it, innocence and trust
came at a high price, but it
   and they didn't destroy me.

I did a lot of praying, and
   making promises for the
future, and questioning if
   they had taken lessons
from my Dad, he had lying
   down to a science!

"Visit a Touch of the Past, Today"

In ankle-length aproned dark cotton frock
   revealing calf-high button shoes,
     she bids me enter the dim, cosy interior.

Plank floors embraced with hand woven rugs,
   hand-turned straight back chairs and
    benches cushioned in colorful prints.
Displaying wreathed artemisia, tansy, mint &
   herb-filled baskets hooked on low beams.
    An aromatic touch of the past.

A tea table gracefully set for the young,
   stage prepared with antique dolls set side
    her collection of shelved picture books.
Unique lace filtered streams of morning light
   spotlight a ceiling-hung framed quilt
   two-thirds complete.
    Challenging skilled hands to continue
     with thimble, needle and thread
    A reminiscence of the past.

Hand-measured leaves steeped in a
   steaming earthenware pot, she pours
    and we sip aromatic tea
     from white spattered on blue,
      Williamsburg cups.
Then munch into thick child-inspired
   gingerbread gems, still warm
    from the wood-burning oven.
     A tasty glimpse of the past.

Hand-dipped tapers await dusk.
   Kerosene lights strategically
      set at attention
as the giant cottonwood steals sunlight
  from our quiet conversation
     linking today with the past.

Featured on the front cover of The Senior's Beacon, Jan. 1992, with a photo of a man and lady dressed in period clothing—riding a bicycle built for two.

Prompt: Describe seeing someone do the extraordinary

Rain had set in for the day the morning we arrived in New Orleans. After driving through the French-Quarter, we decided to visit their well-renowned "Aquarium of the Americas."

People had lined-up from two directions to purchase entry tickets when, like a cloud passing overhead, discussions gradually softened into silent awareness. All eyes were focused on a slender young woman wearing a calf-length beige cape.

Balancing on her left foot, she slipped her right foot out of her loafer and using her toes like nimble fingers, flipped back her cape, and removed her billfold from a trouser pocket. Placing her billfold on the nearby shoulder-high counter, she opened her billfold, counted out the bills needed for her ticket and returned her billfold and ticket in her trouser pocket.

Then, as graceful as a ballet dancer, she slipped her right foot back into her loafer and proceeded inside with her companion, her cape swung closed around her shoulders.

It took the ticket agents and other patrons waiting in line a moment to reasses the reason they were in line.

"Timeless, Dignified, Always In Style"

Growing up, she had always
  cherished his coat,
had even borrowed it
  on more than one occasion.

Once, he found her curled inside
  his over-coat—sound asleep.
more frequently—playing
  dress-up with her friends.

Now...years later...her heart
  bursting with pride.
She knows she can conquer the world!
  He always knew she could.

The gray-plaid drapes her
  shoulders like an old friend
as she lovingly adjusts
  the lapel.

  Ignoring the ankle-length
    drooping kick pleat and
  hem held in place
    with safety pins.
  The missing buttons and
    frayed button holes,
    the pulled-apart pocket-
    seams, belted to keep
      out the cold...

of this wool, plaid top-coat
   her brother left
      her in his will.

"Atlantic Beach"

The North Carolina
   horizon borders infinity.
Milky gray skies
   edge the Atlantic
midst speeding misty clouds.

Storm-churned waves
   undulate, swirl, sidestep,
as rows of continuous
   rippling caps spew forth
frothy peaks of surging
   roars of thunder…
then-dissipate in shy
   silent appeal to the
sandy beach; releasing
   gifts of crusty, polished
shells, pearlescent treasures
   of generations of the
Atlantic's left-over housing.

Mid-morning, clear
   sun-filled skies reflect
the calm Atlantic
   like a shimmering jewel.
An erratic ocean breeze
   kicks about a trembling kite.

Sea gulls swoop
   their bomber-shaped bodies
defy gravity, as they glide in pairs,
   in sixes—alone. Soaring, sweeping,
dipping, catching thermal air currents,
   then grounding on pencil-thin legs
     to a sedate walk.

Their fragile footprints cross-cut
   cool ivory sand, midst
running-shoe scrolls and
   all-terrain vehicle tracks.
Life-prints tomorrow's tide
    will erase.

Prompt: Describe posture of two people and add to the story

While observing two people at the grocery, no matter what the man did as he slowly shuffled behind her, his shoulders hunched forward, the woman who was driving the battery-powered grocery cart was never satisfied.

While she directed the man who appeared to be accompanying her, she was cussing like a longshoreman, and belittling him in any way possible.

I wasn't the only observer who had turned away rather than stop and stare at this train wreck. Even three aisles over, her voice echoed and sent more than one shopper towards the checkout. His patience was beyond belief as her temperament and language lashed at him as she sent him up one aisle and down another, especially when he returned with the wrong brand item.

I was surprised when he stopped in front of me. I was on my tip-toes in an attempt to reach something that I prayed would not hit me on the head before I could snatch it. He smiled at me as he readily took it off the shelf and placed it in my hand. I thanked him and thought, *wow!* When he had to be, he was well over six feet tall.

The man's faded, over-sized starched front creased trousers needed suspenders, as well as a leather belt to hold them up. His shirt was also clean and neatly pressed. The collar and cuffs were badly frayed, but they were well-hidden with layers of starch. The heels of his black, well-polished shoes, were worn down, appearing to be as worn out as he appeared to be. The toes of his shoes were so shiny they reflected the bright ceiling lights off her brilliant necklace too. She was nicely dressed, and it appeared she had never missed a meal, but looked fresh as a daisy from a recent visit to the beauty parlor, as not a hair was out of place.

He followed her to the checkout and when he leaned over to pick out a Hershey bar with almonds and a Bit-o-Honey, his dog-tags swung out of his shirt.

A Marine in full uniform, who was ahead of the woman in line, and had just picked up his gallon of milk, quickly set it down, and announced directly towards Henry, "Atten-Hut!" and saluted.

The suspender-clad man with a well-used "Special Services" beret, quickly removed it from his trousers pocket, and tugged it into place as he straightened to attention—his heels clicking together, and returned the salute.

His faded blue eyes teared-up as he nodded a thank you recognition to the service man who had saluted him. Then Henry handed the cashier his folded small paper sack topped with two one-dollar bills, and the candy bars he was purchasing.

"Henry," the cashier began, recognizing him as a monthly regular. With a gently respectful smile she added, as she handed him his sack with the candy and money left inside, "The Marine who just left paid for your groceries and candy."

He graciously nodded his thank you and struggled into his faded military jacket. Just outside the grocery, a table had been set up for Veteran's Day, handing out Poppies for donations.

"Henry! Come along now!" the woman announced like he was deaf.

"WAIT!" he replied gruffly, as he placed the two one-dollar bills and one candy bar in their bucket, then turned and saluted the officers tending the table. Once he plopped inside the vehicle in the handicap parking space, he leaned his head back, and bowed his head in thanks. Proud. Satisfied he had had a spectacular day.

"I Am You"

I am special! Complex! Different!
   Because…
my birth, my ancestors, my religious belief –
   my experiences, good and bad-
my environment, the people I meet –
   all touch my life,
      leave a mark.

My family, peers, friends, strangers—
   the nucleus is ever-growing.
Today intertwines with yesterday
   surrounding my entire being.

Those I love and those who
   love in return,
those who treat me unjustly
   and my reaction.

I am who I am today—
   continually changing tomorrow.
What I read and how
   I interpret it.

What I hear and accept—
   What I watch, touch and smell—
What I eat and wear—
   is the visible me.

I only pass this way but once,
  a link in God's eternal plan.
Some parts of my puzzle are
  hidden from view.

I am complex and special
  I   AM   YOU.

"Bell's Palsy"

A cranial nerve on the upper-left-side of my brain shorted-out by a Virus and left the nerves on the left side of my face paralyzed.

This happening smoothed-out all the wrinkles on the left-side of my forehead, and face.

The left side of my upper lip felt numb, like when the dentist shoots pain-free meds in a tooth. Thus, this lazy-looking side of the my mouth resulted: in half of my smile being on vacation.

My left eyebrow became stationary and my left eye immovable. In the first days, my eye wouldn't even close. To save my foggy vision, and keep my eye moist since it couldn't blink, an emulsion was needed to keep it moist and protected.

Our body is so miraculous, as it works to repair and reconnect these nerves.

Now—to Recovery—No Pain -
My Lips Twitch—My entire Jaw Jumps: which is best without my dentures because they click so loud and fast, it's like a tap-dancer—on speed.

The nerves on both sides of my face— jerk, jump, tremble, twitch, pulls and

grabs my cheek and tugged it left from
my mouth into my left cheek and held it
for ten seconds, then gently released it.

Took hold of my upper lip and twisted
it around like it was silly-putty. Puckered
my lips like I was sucking on a pickle
soaked in alum.

Slid my jaw to the right—then to the
left a half-dozen times. I could have used
some music.

Just shy of six weeks in recovery, my
Jaw slam-jammed over and over, and up and
down, so fast and hard over one-thousand
times. My head was bouncing up and
down. Afterwards I was exhausted!

Then jerked my tongue straight out,
And then swept my tongue to the right
all the way around my mouth and then
to the left, all the way around. Similar
to a cat washing its whiskers.

Then opened my mouth wide—then
with a slapping sound, released it
against my tongue, like it was a rubber
band.

My right eye blinked so many times
I lost count. Sending messages over to
my left eye which really felt like it did
blink, but I'm not certain if it did.

Some tugs move my mouth side to
side and then sweeps up to my nose
and around up to my right eye.

My nose itches, twitches, and wiggles
like an Easter Bunny commercial on TV.

These movements have been repeated
almost daily. Some sessions have lasted an
hour, two hours—with short breaks in-
between.

Results as of 9-25-2017—I can now chew
my food on the left side. I can drink without
the assistance of two fingers at the left of
my mouth.

Thank heavens for a lipstick brush, but as
of 10-08-2017, I still can't rub my lips
together yet without it being a bit crooked,
but my lips are stronger. And my smile is
back from vacation.

All the wrinkles in my face are back, and
I have watched the wrinkles in my forehead
slowly show-up from the center to far left, and
my left eyebrow is back to normal—moving
up when the right eyebrow raises, dozens of times.

My left eye will close, just not blink yet.
My eye doctor, took pictures
of my eyes and compared to the past six years
it revealed there is no damage to my Retina.

Twitches while I have been typing.

"Unexpected Winner"

A loved of-the-sea tortoise named Tilly
who thought racing a hare was quite silly,
   while flirting with Joe,
    she stubbed her big toe,
flipped over, spinning terrified Tilly!

A fighter when born, she still wasn't done.
Deep down a hidden, slick slope, she then spun,
   hit a tree named Drew,
    like a bird she flew,
right over the hare, then bounced up and won!

Ears drooped, James skidded like a bowling pin,
then bowed, saluting her fantastic win.
   Leaves swirled in a breeze,
    the dust made him sneeze,
then he raced up hill with a silly grin.

GRAY

"Memories Clarified"

While working on
   my memoir titled
"How Writing Changed
   My Life", I credit

my Mom for dating
   and identifying
people, and places
   where a photo was

taken—on the photos—
   that brought to
life reminders that
   clarified moments
and refreshed
   happenings.
Also thanks for the
many times the

Lord held my hand,
   and still guides
my thoughts
   and prayers.

Marilyn, Mom, Carol, Susie

"A Letter to My Mom"

After the divorce, you were
   awarded custody of us, your
three daughters, Marilyn,
   Susan, and Carolyn. I finished
fourth grade at a one-room
   school house. The lady of the
house didn't like us at all, and
   was ready for us to move-
along before school was out

The summer between the fourth
   and fifth grade, we stayed a few
nights in Grandma Ruth's apartment
   at the fifteen-room Central House
Hotel in Continental, that your mom's
   family had leased and owned in the
early 1900's. It may have been named
   The Pease Hotel at some point. Later,
it was renamed the Peg Leg.

It was still spring when we moved
   into a house in the country between Continental and Dupont,
   Ohio. I was excited. The nearby
farmer offered to pay me to ride on
   a tomato planter in the field close to
the house you were renting.

There were two round metal ground-
   level seats, with a place for another
girl and myself to put our feet. When
   the water gushed into a hole in the
dirt—we stuck a tomato plant in the

ground of the bumpiest ride ever—
   even over some huge clumps of dirt
as the tractor pulled the planter back
   and forth across acres of this plowed
field. My first paying job. But one day
   at that wage was enough for me.

The following month of 1944, my little
sisters stayed with your mom, and
you and I spent the summer, in a
one-room apartment on South Main
Street in Lima. You worked in a counter-
service restaurant next door to the
Wagon-Wheel.

That fall, you moved us girls in with a
a distant cousin and her family who
lived on a farm in Jackson Township.
While living here, I attended the fifth
grade and Susie the first grade at LaFayette.
I'm not complaining, but moving must
not be something that leaves a lasting
impression with me.

When Dad and his mother, visited this cousin's
House, Susie climbed a tree and refused
to come down until they left, however
before they left Grandma insisted you
had to move us out of that house because
they had a teenage son and that
wouldn't be safe for me. Really?

Who moved us from the farmhouse to
a furnished cottage owned by your
Aunt Hazel who lived in Lima? The
cottage was located in Island View
across the road from a boat ramp of
Indian Lake. I attended grade six and
Susie grade two, at Lakeview.

The fall of 1945-1946, you had found a
  better paying job, and we had just
moved into a house in Lima -- where
  we not only lived together, but you had
hired two different ladies to take care
  of us while you were at work.

However you made the mistake of filing
  for help from children's services, because
now you had to pay for rent, as well as,
  childcare, and they went after Dad for
not paying child support.

Then Dad and his mother, Emmie, contacted
  the head of Allen County Children's Welfare
Department. Dad decided he would was not
  going to pay one more dime to you, Mom.
He LIED! He said all he had to prove was that
  we were alone—when we weren't—and he
could file for custody. He LIED! The court
  listened. Believed him. Court records
showed this.

  I do not recall Dad or Grandma visiting
    us in Lima. Nor Children's Services coming
  while you were at work, and forced us to leave
  with them.

Years later, your three daughters contacted
  the Allen County Children's Services, regarding
our records. They had taken a photo of us that
  day. Their files described me as belligerent and un-

cooperative. But you know after reading our file
   I questioned what did they expect?

 Mom, you and my sisters were counting on me!
   These strangers were taking us away and I had
no way of contacting you, and neither did those ladies
   watching us either. To this day I can't recall being taken.

When people hear my story, their comment is—well
   that was another time. Meaning what? Why or when
is it okay for the man to act like he is single, but the
   woman should know her place is in the Home?
Plus—you never said one unkind word about our Dad
   to us—your girls.

But I have comments from more than one
   family member who mentioned that Dad
was seldom home and was running with more
   than one woman for practically all the years
he was with you. So. I am curious. Is this why
   your oldest brother was staying with us
for a part-time job, but didn't want to see
   you be alone when Susie was born.

Plus a couple of years later, after you delivered
   Carol at home by yourself while you were
on the phone with the doctor, and he later
   made a house call. Dad moved us into town
while Carol was still a baby, and your next
   brother had come and stayed with us for
awhile. Did he also come to take care of you?

The Allen County Children's Home Administrator's
   Office was walnut colored wood paneling. He
asked me a lot of questions. I was so petrified, I
   have no idea what I said.

Us three girls took our research to Seneca
   County, where you and dad's divorce
took place. Recently I shredded my copy of those
divorce records, including letters your mom had
   written to the courts because she was

concerned that you might have a nervous
   breakdown. No wonder! You arrived home
from work and your children were gone and
no one could or would tell you where we were.
   That had to have been one of your darkest days.

According to the records, we were at the Allen
   County Children's Home for about six weeks.
I don't recall if they allowed you to see us there.
   The photos of you at the Van Wert County Fair
on Labor Day 1947, would have been just two
   weeks after we were taken to the Flat Rock
Children's Home tells a story. I like to think you
   knew where we were by then.

I read somewhere they sent you a bill for our
   care while we were there. During this time
there was another court hearing in Tiffin.
You never talked about any of this to us, so I
   can't write about it, but dad's second wife, sent

me a letter years later, and said that they,
   (meaning dad and her) knew they had made
a lot of mistakes with us girls.

Several family members were interested in taking
   us in, but didn't have enough rooms. Then, Dad
decided if he couldn't have us—no one could!
   Even several of his sisters wanted us. This proved
to me that the person making the loudest noise—
   with the deepest pockets and in reflection—
caused the greatest pain to you, Mom and your girls.

But he still never made an effort to change
   anything. Anyhow this letter may have been
in response to my letter after my first baby was
   born—asking dad's permission to take Susie
and Carol out of The Children's Home. Of course he
   said 'NO'. I had learned from Seneca County
Children's Services that I had to ask dad if
   I could leave The Children's Home and come
and live with you after graduation because
   I wasn't eighteen yet—before the county would
approve of it. They didn't want to deal with him again.

Odd, that I do recall ole' Mr. Jensen and a woman
   from Children's Services in Tiffin arriving in
Lima and delivering Susie, Carol and me to The
   Flat Rock Ebenezer Evangelical United Brethren
Children's Home in Seneca County, Ohio.

It was six weeks before you were allowed to visit us.
  I need to add this. Even though we were much further
away from you, the Flat Rock home was owned and run
  by the church, and so much nicer than the previous one.

The Lord and his angels were no doubt kept busy
  but I finally felt safe, even though it was hard to
see you leave after every visit. Carol remembers
  the other girls would crowd around you because
we were blessed to have a mom who came to visit.
  Few had family that visited. You were twenty-nine.
Your girls were not in their teens yet.

If I had it to do over…I wish I had asked you where
  you lived all those times when we were separated.
But like life—you died long before even we could
  have contemplated you would.
But where did you live all these years Mom when
  you found friends and family to take care of us?
Did you also live with friends? How did you survive
  as a single mom with Dad not paying support? You
were juggling work and paying for child care, food
  and a place to live on a waitress's income. This
had to be a very lonely, scary time.

You said you once cleaned house for a friend named
  Esther who had her dance studio in her home. Did
she offer you a place to stay? George told me after
  we were put in the home, that had he known
what Dad planned, he would have taken all of us
  out of state. He also told me that you worked as a

winder for electric motors in Westinghouse. Later, you
worked on a production line at Lima Electric. And
that a couple of friends, helped you out. Because
you couldn't keep up on the production line, because
you had went back to work two weeks early after
major surgery. I now understand that 'piecework'
meant more pay for more parts per day than was
expected.

Since you didn't own a car—you either walked, rode
the city bus, caught a ride with a co-worker or with
George. But still you managed to purchase a double lot
on Adams Street in Lima, where you later moved your
little mobile home you had purchased and had once
parked at George's sister's house for a while.

Stepdad George, Susie, Marilyn, Carol

Until recently, I didn't realize this had been a concern
of mine all these years. I really did like your compact
and tidy mobile home though, Mom. It was ALL yours.
Finally. A place of your own. You look proud in the photo.

But as in all your three hour, monthly visits to see us,
there was a look of distant resignation in your eyes.
However I do have a photo of the two of us taken on the
evening of my graduation, we both are really smiling.
Finally. You had one of your daughter's back to live with you.

Marilyn & Mom, graduation night

You had just started dating George at the time we were
taken from you. I remembered his car. Then later, the
two of you married and built a home on this same lot.

Through prayer and thanksgiving, although you never mentioned the 'nitty-gritty' of such a painful memory of your first marriage, I now understand why when you were in the hospital with the cancer when Dad's mother came to the hospital to see you. George's sister, was sitting with you at the time, flipped when they introduced themselves, and told them 'She doesn't want to see you!' (I had no idea—at the time—why she was so angry and stomped out of the room.)

In hindsight thanks for doing your very best. I wish you would have felt you could talk to us. But I'm so very thankful you got the chance to see some of your grandchildren born.

Remember when during one of our 'window-shopping down-town Lima Days', we stopped by Kresge's counter for a hot chocolate? We were just finishing up when a nearby couple's loud remarks erupted in yelling? The woman was in tears. And he said something that apparently hit a nerve with you, because you left a dime tip for the waitress and literally pushed me out the door ahead of you.

I've not forgotten what you said when you and George helped me sign up for classes at Northwestern School of Commerce, weeks before I graduated from high school and also bought me a new dress for graduation. Paid my Greyhound bus ticket from Bellevue to Lima—plus a job interview with the owners of the Big Wedge who were anxious to set my hours to coincide with my classes—plus the city bus dropped me at the Wedge after classes, which was not one of their regular stops. (What you didn't know was the nurse and cook at the home put together a paper bag lunch to take with me on the bus, because I only had two dollars to my name, for emergencies.)

Your comment: 'Remember. Men can cheat on their spouses for years, and years and years! But the wife better not, for spite, or payback or retaliation ever step out even once. I want my daughters to get a good education, so you won't be trapped in a marriage-gone-wrong with no escape.'

Just so you know, I do not blame you for anything that happened. More than once I have been asked, 'Don't you hate your parents for putting you in a children's home?'
"My reply, No. I refuse to carry around anger that was not of my making. It cannot be un-done."
Actually which reminded me, first off of something that happened before guests arrived for my wedding shower. I was in the dining room behind the partial divider just a few steps inside your front door section of

your living room. So I was out of sight of whoever had knocked on your front door. I couldn't see them and they couldn't see me. However it became apparent this was one unexpected guest that was not welcome.

I heard you what? You threw the lock on your storm door and said, 'No. You can't see her! Leave her alone! I can't believe you had the nerve to even stop by my house! Leave!'

I was surprised you didn't slam the inside door, but the tone
   in your voice was so full of pain and a boatload of anger,
that I turned away so you wouldn't know I had heard that
   exchange.

You took a few deep breaths although I had noticed
   your hands
   were shaking just before I turned away. However a nearby
mirror revealed you were near the type of sad, gut-wrenching tears
   as a result of the appearance of one's worst nightmare.
   I wish
you would have felt you could talk with your daughters.
   But at least you found happiness with George.

"A Pickled Patience Personified Promise"

To fulfill a
  someday promise,
I requisitioned an
  exclusive, unique,
fashionable wheel-
  chair that will
fit my sister's
  suggestions and
requests.

It breaks
  my heart that
she is not residing
  where she
occasionally dreams
  of living—in the
home of her choice.

Thirteen surgeries
  failed to correct a
rare birth defect—a
  split retina. She was
born with only 1/8th
  of her cornea. Two
transplants failed. Her
  eyes are permanently
dilated, and altered from
  pear shape to round.

She enjoys reading the
  newspaper with pre-
scription lenses, plus a
  magnifying glass held
against her nose. People
  on her television screen
are life-size.

It would be amazing, if
  an artist could sketch
what she does see.
  Better yet, if she could
sketch what she sees.
Like me sitting on
  top of my hat.
Or, during the drive to
  her eye appointment,
she saw a man waving
  a flag—directing
traffic—perched on
  top of a light pole.

Tear-filled giggles and
  chuckles followed,
because she knew neither
  made any sense.

Her optometrist added,
  "I'd never doubt what
you see. It's just a
  miracle that you do."

Steadfast to a fault,
   she continues to
persevere through
   these perplexing,
frustrating happenings—
   but is also quick to
smile, forgive, apologize.

So is it any wonder,
   Lord, why her
memories are some-
   times momentarily
scrambled with reality?
Baffling, to say the least?

And has she not
   questioned since
childhood, why no
   one else sees what
she sees—the way—she
   sometimes sees it?

She invested every
   dime he left her—
thinking, what if she
   lost the chance to
see, and needed
   help some day?

Resigned that she is
   destined to spend

the rest of her life in
　yet another
institution—thankfully
　her number is not
the same as her children's
　home number was from
age five thru fifteen.

Even with a high-school
　diploma, jobs for
her were scarce. And
　although she never
could acquire a license
　to drive a car—she at
least deserves to pedal,
　wheel, or be pushed in
the Lincoln/Cadillac of
　wheelchairs, A gift
from her second Dad.

Marilyn's sister Carol

"Photographs"

Forgotten happenings
   are stopped and held,
by the shutter of
   father time.

Remembrances
   of happy times
are once again
   revealed, of

holidays and birthdays
   family gatherings
meals, vacations and
   far-away-places.

School, church, sports
   activities, and awards.
What fun it is to travel
   through life's pathway

of yesteryear and relive
   treasured moments
in photographs old
   and new.

"Sisters, Differences and Connections"

Because I was the eldest or
   perhaps because our Mom
was also the eldest of five,
   I also wore the automatic
baby-sitter/mom/sister hat.

When I wasn't quite three, I was
   holding my baby brother in my
arms, in a big rocking chair, in the
   dark of night, while the house
where we lived—burned down.

Mom took three-year old Susie
   shopping and left six-month old
Carol with six-year old me. There
   are pictures of the three of us -
as we aged, but I will be forever

thankful that one of mom's requests
   was honored when we were admitted
to the Flat Rock Children's Home.
   Keep my daughters together. If
someone wants to adopt one –

they have to take all three. Neither the
   State, nor the administration were
required to honor her request. There
   were times when people were
interested in one, but not all three.

The hardest part about leaving the
   Children's home on graduation
night, was that I couldn't take them
   with me, nor could Mom and George.
Although, the Big & Little Girls

were in the same building, we
   didn't live in the same quarters.
I started in the seventh grade
   but slept in the Big Girls
dormitory. My sisters were together

in the Little Girls' Dormitory and
   were always close. My 'jobs' kept me
busy, and even though we ate in
   the same dining room, we sat at
different tables. I always knew where

they were, so I still wore the
   Mom/sister hat. But oddly enough
when Mom came to visit the second
   Sunday of each month, moments I
remember as we watched together

in the doorway of the Archway as her
   vehicle drove away. We didn't talk.
We just watched in silence. Then
   separated, as they went back to the
Little Girls' basement/playroom and I

went up a dozen steps to the Big Girls'
   quarters. The office no doubt handed
any gifts Mom may have brought to their
   Matron to mark with their number.
I put mine away in my closet or dresser
   and combed my

hair to go to the Main Building Kitchen
   to assist getting the evening meal ready.
Not much to do because it was Sunday
   evening. The main meal had been around
noon. From habit I always held visiting

day with our Mom as a warm blessing.
   We were in the very small percent who
had anyone come to visit. So leaving
   graduation night was not easy. But I
at least had a place to go. Not everyone

did. A month before graduation, Mom
   set it up for me to take the Greyhound
bus ride to Lima, by myself—which wasn't
   easy. But I had signed-up for business college.
   Mom had set up an interview for me

at the Big Wedge which wasn't very
   far from Mom and George's house.
They served breakfast, burger's and
   fries and Chicken in the Basket, plus
home deliveries and curb-side-service

in the summer. State Route 81 and 25
  were busy and Schoonover Park and
Swimming Pool was busy in the summer.
  Business fell off after I-75 opened.
Mom and George drove me back to the

children's home on Sundays. My schooling
  wasn't finished yet. My visits back to see
my sisters have become a blur. I worked
  when I wasn't attending class.

After I was married, we tried to take
  my sisters out of the home, but our
Dad wouldn't sign the papers. However, Dad
  signed so Carol was allowed to leave when
Susie graduated. So she finished school
  locally.

However, I had promised Mom I would
  be there with her, when Children's Services
came to the house. She was so nervous, truly
  afraid to know what to say, and when I
helped her, the representative for
  Children's Services didn't like me helping

Mom—and huffed and puffed and demanded
  to know how I knew about all this. I gave
her my name and she remarked, "We have
  no record of you." She lied. This rep's attitude
was formed before she arrived. I had read

that we are all just a number and names in
   a file. Oh, yes. They even had taken a photo
of the three of us as well the day they stole us
   from our mom, because they could—because
we saw all this when we went looking for
   our records. On a lighter note,
   all three of us girls have kept in touch.

We haven't lived that far apart. All
   three of us were married when
Mom died. Susie even borrowed
   my wedding dress. One day Susie
called me about why she wanted a

certain picture she had purchased
   at a neighbor's porch sale. It looked
familiar to me as well. While searching
   through some old photographs, I
found the same photo on our Mom's

mom's dining room wall. Years later,
   I acquired some pictures from a
family member who had purchased
   a house to use as a rental. One was a
duplicate of a photo titled, 'Girl on a

Bench'. I had looked at it daily on the
   Little Girls' living room wall. Another
surprise was during a visit at Susie's
   house as I stopped in her bedroom.
I said, "Your one wall in blue wall-

paper, is the same design as the rose
in my hallway at home." Susie said,
"Wait until you see Carol's living room
in the same pattern in a soft green."

As one can tell, we did not shop
together, but were still amazed how
we made other similar choices in life.

A belated thank you to Our Mom for
asking that we be kept together.

Susie, Marilyn, Carol

"Two Little Girls"

My Sisters, were you see—
   locked in a dark closet, small—
punished for their childish prank.
   Why they'd dared to peek—

from beneath the stairs to
   maybe see if it was true, indeed,
does matron really wear men's
   underwear?

Note: This was kept a secret from me for years.

"A Step Father"

George,
   I've looked high and low
   hither and yon, for a clue—
but nowhere could I find,
   a card I felt was true.

With a story or message sincere
   for a father—who is not,
well, legally, you see—but is
   100%—from the heart.

You listen to my questions,
   problems and complaints,
from a broken heart, to how to
   mend doors, pipes and plates.

So. This is to say Happy Birthday,
   Merry Christmas to Father's Day
all rolled into one. With a very
   special thank you—for
     marrying my Mom.

George & Marilyn's mom

"George was Creative"
*I read this poem at George's funeral
and later found his lost infant Baptismal Papers*

George was creative—innovative,
  a master at finding ways to
do a two-man job by himself.

Such as, welded a length of pipe
  onto a particular wrench…
and glued two clamps back to
  back, so he could reach the
unreachable, by himself.

Although he was a very
  private person, in his 83
years—he was also, a mentor
  teacher, student. Yet wasn't
bashful about asking questions
  he needed answers to.

Yet, with a sly wink, took the
  time to tease young and old—
which usually brought smiles.

However, struggled with proving
  himself to his Dad—until finally
when he and his brother, Ralph
  finished building George & Edna's
home—his Dad gave his approval.

What greater friends can you have?
   A friend bought his house and
another bought his beloved
   Dodge truck.
Rev. Doug Adams added, George's
   dearest friend Dick was the
only person invited when George
   was baptized in his Room at
Cridersville's Otterbein in Ohio.

"Grieving and Thanksgiving"

*My sister Susie and Stepfather,
George died 16 days apart.
Thirty days later…*

What was happening?
  My chest felt as fluttery as
    a gentle trapped breeze
      which escalated
and sent my blood pressure
      soaring.

like the back and forth whispering
  delicacy of a butterfly
      settling
on a billowing blade of grass,
     balancing
with the strength of a ballet dancer—
  unsettled…unnerved,
    seeking answers.

All right, Jesus!—What will be!
    Will be!
  I need your help here!
I can't change what's happened!
  I need your guidance…
    and *found calming in
      meditation…*

Blessings bathed with love
   and support were like
      morning sunshine.
Fulfilling the expectations,
   and accepting the decisions,
and choices that I had no control
   over was a revelation.

I just needed to get it together
   and thankfully…
      trust my heart
         and the Lord.

"Susie, Until we meet again…"

We create our OWN memories…
   Fall, Winter, Spring, Summer.

But not all are within our realm to create.
   Some things just happen.

Fall is the season of changes
   as leaves fall in colorful disarray
marking time when life's circle is put in order—
   in preparation for next season's glory
and another chance to get it right.

Unlike dying—when there are
   no second chances,
only breathless good-byes
   until someday we meet again
through a spectrum of imperfect sunrises
   and peaceful, forgiving sunsets.

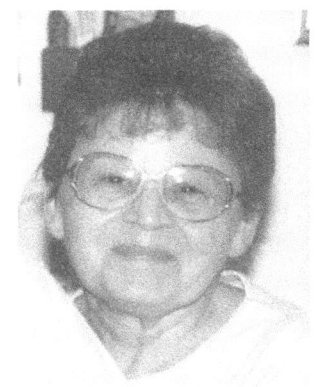

Susie

"Susie"

Her birth was
   difficult, but she fought
insistently—with the
   strength of an army.

Filled with stubborn
   mischievousness in
her sparkling eyes
   and innocent smile,

she was quick to judge
   with a double-edged
sword - slower to forgive—yet
   compassionate to a fault.

Distance isn't always a
   matter of miles, of
time, but circumstance—
   and the unsuspecting
were left wondering why.

Proud and protective of
   those she loved. With
profound tenacity, stitched
   designs for timely gifts -
in cross-stitch.

She never forgot a birthday
   proclaiming our sister ties,

and untiringly researched our
  missing genealogy links.

She battled pain in silence
  even when it became a
close companion, but cancer
  won that battle.

And she left an empty space
  in the middle, but not
forgotten. "How can I live
  without her?" baby sister
murmured. "She is too much
a part of me."

Susie

"Going Home"

We never know when
  we leave our home,
if we'll ever be able
  to come home again.

When Mom was whisked away
  in an ambulance, I leaned down
and kissed her on the cheek.
  "Don't tell George I'm scared,"
she whispered.
  This was to be our 'goodbye'.

Although they took X-rays, after
  X-rays, there was no recognition.
George took her home for
  Mother's Day Week, but nothing
was ever the same. The cancer had
  destroyed her memory.

After weeks in a coma,
  life support was suspended.
Her strong heart—her breath
  silenced—her spirit freed,
for the Lord had been waiting.

*My sister, Susie struggled
  to breathe, but continued
to smoke for several years.
  Hospitalized with Lung Cancer.

After surgery and thirty days in
   ICU, she was released to her
daughter's home. Not her own.

Hospice took charge and she
   never opened her eyes, yet
spoke a few words to calm
   Paula's puppy.

*George, our stepdad, fell
   out of bed. Transported by
Cridersville's EMTs to the
   hospital. Later, to Otterbein
Assisted Living; but he
   wanted to go home. So he
planned, practiced, and
   worked hard to go back home.

But once there, he quickly tired
   of struggling with a walker.
After two days, Easter Sunday morn
   he called me and said, "Come and
get me, Kid. I'm afraid I will mess-up
   on my meds, being here alone.

Thus he was satisfied with making
   Otterbein Assisted Living his home.
Don and I took him to doctors'
   appointments, and he proudly
paid for our lunch as a thank you.

He sat under a shade tree in the backyard of his old home, and watched
his household goods sold at auction,
   by Amy, 'a lady auctioneer'. Later -
a friend bought his home and another
   friend bought his beloved truck.
"I'm living like a 'King', Kid. He
   passed the following October.
Ten days after my Sister, Susie.

*My baby Sister, Carol smoked when
   Mom didn't tell her & Susie not to.
Then battled anxiety for over forty years
   and said she needed script for XANAX.
She tripped over her blanket and fell
   backwards, hitting her head hard
twice. No wonder her body and mind
   trembled when the ER Team ran tests,
interspersed with questions. Machines
   results of her brain, were read.
Doctors were puzzled—comparing
   percentages. Looking for answers.

No mention was made of the fact that
   she was suffering from a highly
infectious U.T I. No wonder she was
   confused! In addition to this—she
was also in a lot of pain from her two
   falls resulting in a fractured vertebrae.

XANAX was taken away, with
   nothing in its place. She was awake
for three days and two nights—
   talking gibberish non-stop. They
said her brain was swelled.

Plied with numerous drugs,
   Doctors trying to find a "fix."
When placed in psychiatric care,
   nurses picked her up to place
her on a gurney for further testing.
   Her body was like that of a
broken doll made of straw.

She was moved from place to
   place. Room to room. Strangers
asking more questions. Strangers
   ordering her—you can't get out
of bed by yourself. Take these pills.
   Two she refused because she
knew they would make her ill.

XANAX—by prescription only. Her
   Doc had told her they were not
addictive. Now she may never go
   back to her pride and joy—her
home. She grew-up in a children's
   home. Spending her final years in
an institution would surely break
   her heart.

She was placed in a nursing home,
   for rehab. Can her feisty spirit battle
the trial and error meds, searching
   a brain still in turmoil, still needing
healing. With daytime meds her sharp
   understandable thoughts spilled
out at high speed. Yet she is bored,
   disconnected, without her cell phone.

Possibly in six to twelve months…
   when the XANAX is finally swept away.
Perhaps then her brain can create new
   Neurons—and realign their Network
with bright new circuits.

But she can't ever go home—to live
   alone, but is well enough to move
into Assisted Living. And she did well
   in this new home, away-from-home.
She was crocheting some really nice
   Doilies. Then they moved her to
another room and area (to make room
   for someone else), where she felt out
of place, and she changed.

She quit: crocheting and listening to music,
   watching her 60" TV, playing a hand or
two of cards, and most important of all
   interacting positively with family, or
reading a book, the newspaper, her iPad,
   working on her family history and
photos. She gave up.

Carol

Now, the rest of the story.
   Carol was born with so
many complications with
   her eyes—no one at the hospital

asked about her eye drops—
   until I insisted.
At birth, the pupil of her eyes were
   pear-shaped instead of
round. Her Retinas were
   split and she only had a
miniscule percentage
   of her cornea.

As a child, one of her
   assigned jobs at the
children's home was to
   push one of the mowers.

Years later, she admitted
   the other kids yelled at
her because she never
   mowed straight—how

could she see, especially
   on a sunny day, but she
graduated high school.
   She researched our family

Genealogy. She played games
   on her iPhone, and
crocheted clothes for
   dolls of all sizes—

even when what she was
   seeing, wasn't at all
reality. Even after having
   thirteen surgeries

on her eyes. One left her
   eyes permanently
dilated. She tried wearing
   glasses, even contacts—

but scar tissue
   kept the contacts
from staying in place.

She and her husband
   raised a family of four,

and although she never
   could drive a car, she

was always teasing me
   she was ready to drive.
One day when I drove her
   to see our eye doctor,

I asked her to tell him
   what she was seeing.
"You are sitting on your hat."
She laughed, and added,
"I know you're not."
   Dr. Mark said, "I'll never
doubt what you see, but
   it's a miracle that you do."

Marilyn's mom

"Enduring the Loss of a Child"

My Mom was married at fifteen.
   Gave birth to a baby girl
at sixteen, and two years

later, a little boy was born.
   She struggled daily, as his
defective duodenum brought
   up more of her nutritious

milk than he kept down. Months
   later, she carried him on a
pillow because his alabaster
   skin was tearfully fragile.

Then one day she placed her
   sleeping son in his cradle and
stepped outside to speak to
   someone and when she returned

found he had died, just two days
   before his first birthday. He was
buried in the cemetery between the
   drive and the stone wall.

Two weeks later, his Dad bought
   a lot in this cemetery for his son
but didn't share this information
   with anyone. Many years later,

Johnnie's three sisters found a
   pink gravestone like their Mom
had always wanted and it was
   placed on the space his Dad had

purchased sixty years earlier.
   We asked why they didn't try
surgery? Dad's reply was, "The
   doctor wouldn't guarantee any-

thing. Have your children checked,
   and then asked, "What would you
do?" My reply was, "Even today, they
   make no guarantees, but let you know
what could happen if we have the
   surgery and if we don't. The
decision to do nothing, haunted
   them their entire life.

Years later, I learned that my
   Mom's younger brother had

A first born son who was born with
the same birth defect—

congenital pyloric stenosis.
Their doctor went into Butch's
duodenum—straightened it,
and he survived to raise a
family of his own.

Mom seldom spoke about her
son, but when she held her
grandbabies I am certain it
brought back memories—

however, she had one request,
don't take a picture of
your babies when they
are sleeping.

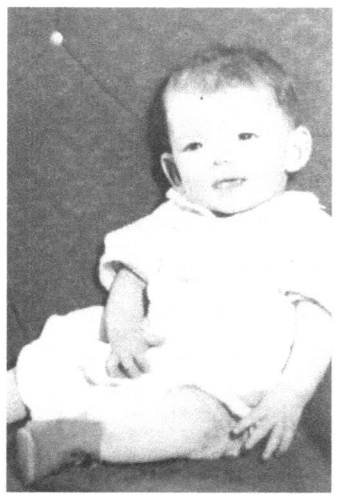

Marilyn's brother John

"Sisters Visit"

Her empty world
  reflects nothing new,
but searches for the
  light that's missing,
never to return?

So like a fragile china
  tea cup one wants
to hold close. Offer
  strength and support.
Find recognition of the

warm sparkle of sharing,
  remembering, loving
trust. But life has dealt
  just one too many
mountains to conquer.

However, the result of
  forty years of meds for
anxiety, has polished-off
  seventy years of
her memory.

No wonder she doesn't
  know me in 2019—her
world is stuck in 1946. But,
  she smiled and got excited
when she saw a photo of me

at eleven years old and cried,
   "That's my sister, Marilyn!"
Now I wonder how long
   she has been looking for
others in the wrong era.

"Dolls in Crochet, Leather and Lace"

I have a space on
   my family room wall,
titled 'Sisters'. But we
   each put our own

touch to porcelain nickel
   dolls and shared with
each other. Carol crocheted
   ecru outfits, head-

bands and moccasins.
   Susie dressed hers in
Indian style clothes of
   ecru leather and mine

to exchange were sewn
   in lace, ribbon and trim.
I made Susie's in blue,
   Carol's in pink, bonnet

and all, my own in white.
   I inherited theirs which
are on display now
   together, even
though we are not.

"I Heard the Bells on Christmas Day"

I heard your voice on Christmas Day
   your heartfelt joy and smile did say,
there's no place like home, dear
   there's no place like home.

Oh, my how you've grown,
   taller and taller, I do declare
but you're not gray yet,
   how can that be?
Why only yester year—
   you were but a babe,
a toddler, on my knee.

Now please—play us a song.
   Everyone join in now
the music is ready
   the piano fine-tuned
just a moment now, please
   let's all sing along.

With misty eyes, she whispered,
   harmony, oh, what harmony!
The blessed angels in heaven
   must be singing backup.

"My Rainbow"

Life is a collection of geometric patterns
   from sunrise to sunset as
contrasting hours fill the day.
   Each is a one time, once-only design.

Today is today.
   It can only become a memory.
Some best forgotten—
   Some to save and cherish.

Others just plain grays.
   Routine in fashion
 Lost in time.
   With just one exception—

Don,
   Each moment
with you
   is a Rainbow.

"March 1st Promised Snow but I Stole Off To Paradise"

Ignoring the steadily falling
   snow piling up outside, I
closed the drapes, settled with
   a fragrant cup of Kona coffee,
and revisited the blended
   cultural spirit of the Islands of
Hawaii, on video cassette.

We departed the plane and were
   greeted with a lei of orchids,
enjoyed a shaded, refreshing, lush
   green Rain Forest, inhaled the
scent of Plumeria Blossoms and
   fields of pineapple.

We stopped at the Road-to- Hana, Maui
   waterfalls. Stepped onto black lava
rock, circling reflective shallows o'er
   a black-sand cove. Strolled under a
Banyon tree that now fills a
   city block in Lahaina, Maui.

Hula dancers danced the language
   of the heart, ukulele and drums—
background for a scrumptious Luau on
   Wailea, Maui Beach at sunset.

Mid-morning, wind-surfers arrived to
  Catch enough wind to fill their sails—
towards Kihei, Maui shore. As the sun sets,
  a slight breeze steals a beach-comber's hat.

However, be cautious of the treachery of
  Oahu's North Side. Only the strong attempt
to challenge these thundering, continuous
  20' waves. Men were swept off their feet,
tumbled about, and spit back on the beach.

The slack-key guitar was initiated by the
  Spanish-speaking cowboys of Hawaii,
in-rhythm with the trade winds gently
  swaying through coconut filled Palms.
Oahu's memorial cemeteries:
  Pearl Harbor, Punchbowl, and
Diamond Head leaves one
  with a sobering feeling. Not
everything here is Paradise.
  Aloha
    Until we meet again.

Marilyn & Don

"Life is a Timeless Momentous Journey"

Is it mapped out in advance by
   some higher power?
Can you help me out with
   this one Lord?

While collecting photos,
   of moments caught
on film—a microcosm
   of memories shared—
      one-time events.

Reveals the result of choices
   others made while
on their journey. The choices
   we make every day. The
connection we make with others—
   just in passing.

How we react to others actions
   is part of what and
who we are.

It is not for others
   to pass judgement,
but take the time
   to appreciate and be
thankful for the moments
   we are granted.

"Our World Had Stopped"

Our world had stopped
　and focused on how
Don was breathing.
　As it diminished, his
blood pressure was at'
　zero, his oxygen at 46,
yet he still watched Ohio
　State beat Michigan and,
had some witty comments
　to add:

When the daughter-in-law
　from Michigan, applauded
when Michigan made a
　touchdown, he motioned
that she could leave.

Later, when Ohio State
　made a touchdown, he
raised his arm in the air,
　and yelled, "Yeah!"

"Hey Dad, look at this picture
　of us at Sean's wedding.
Remember, this is your
　daughter asking—who
Is the prettiest lady here?"
　"Your mom."

"Hey Dad, you know you
   have lots of grandkids
and great grandkids."
   "They're adopted."

How frustrating it must
   have been to just lie there
in the hospital bed, in our
   family room and not be
able to make eye contact
   with those he loved.

When we called family to come,
   that Don could hear them,
and if they wanted to talk to
   him, they best stop by. Our
driveway and yard must have
   looked like a mall parking lot.

One nephew, left a team of
   men working in his kitchen
and rushed out so fast, he
   left his billfold on the table.

After his private moment with
   Grandpa, Scott walked back
into our kitchen, smiling. When
   asked what he had told
Grandpa, he said, "I told him
   I had just made three
Hole's-in-One, and I did it with

Yellow Balls." (Knowing that
Grandpa used yellow balls.)

But, when one guest arrived
   and over-stayed her welcome,
and kept saying, "He needs me."
   when the room was filled
with his children. We were
   courteous, and quiet, but
she finally left, and he said, "I
   thought she would never leave!"

And when one friend-of-the-
   family's minister stopped by,
and loudly pronounced that
   everyone (these were family
who were merely sitting quietly
   in the room) "Leave and let
this man get some rest!"

No one orders anyone from
   our home. We felt blessed
when my daughter's minister
   stopped by—at her request.

"Dearly Beloved"
Read at his funeral

Dearly Beloved,
   It's only been 24 hours
and I miss you already.
   How does one say Goodbye
to someone who had the
   courage to deal with me?

You allowed me to be me—
   never questioned—
always trusted: my instincts,
   my writing, my curiosity
to try something new.

We traded places as
   point-guard with our
children. Together our
   love of music led us to
the Dance Floor.

We shared our joy of travel
   with family and friends;
especially our children
   and grandchildren.

But I don't believe we'll
   ever truly say Goodbye,
for kindred spirits
   seldom travel alone.

The Angels surely felt
   welcome in our full
house, as we sang
   together to the
cranked-up toe-tapping
   love-of-Jesus music.

I know honey, I silently
   prayed, and asked—
"Please, take him home,
   Lord." For you had been
brave, strong, and
   struggled to breathe for
many, many months.

And like a thunderbolt
   from the blue, you
just slipped away.

In the blink of an eye
   your warm rosy skin
quickly faded to but
   a shell, and you left
us with memories
   few live to achieve.

"It was Monday Evening"

It was Monday evening,
   November 10, 2014.
Randy and Lin were seated
   across the room. I was in the
chair beside Don's bed. Sean and
   Christal were lying on the floor.

I woke Sean because Don's
   mouth was open wide in a
continual struggle for air.
   Sean went back to sleep.

I had just thought this prayer,
   "Please take him home, Lord."
That thought was instantaneously
   answered. There was a huge,
loud whooshing sound. Then an
   un-believably shocking stillness.

I laid my hand on his still warm
   chest and yelled, "He's gone!
He's gone!" And I was
   immediately joined in the
loving circle of our children,
   our arms around each other
as we cried, comforting
   each other.

Sean shut-off the oxygen, and we
   all looked at the time. It was
11:30 pm. I called Hospice and
   a Hospice Nurse came
immediately.

Strangely, when she and the funeral
   home rep asked, "Do you need
more time with him: all of us
   replied, "NO". We knew our time
with him had abruptly ended,
   moments earlier.

Then in the confusion of deciding
   the least complicated door to
remove his earthly body, zipped
   in a black body bag—now loaded
on the gurney—from our
   family room.

We helped with directions as they
   carried him out the patio door
and into the chilling black night.

Shock kept the scream inside me,
   for what I saw—still haunts me
to this day…His alabaster profile,
   his lifeless head protruded outside of the black bag, and his head
   wobbled back and forth—like a
plaster bust on a shelf…and I still

wonder if the Lord meant for me
to see…that the Spirit, the Life, of
the man who had so many times
told me he loved me—all those
61 years…Really was Gone!
Wow! What a Revelation!

"Dreams & Dancing"

My former
  destination dreams
have been
  re-routed.

I have had to
  expand my
garden of courage
  and self-reliance

bravely fill the
  silence with
captivating songs
  and the ever-

changing, patience,
  dancing without
a partner
  but with the

Lord's support
  I'll just
dance alone.

"How are You Doing?"

I'm OK. But I have my
  moments. When our
song comes on the
  radio, memory tears
flow like lava, and I
  miss your magical
touch—

the instantaneous
  response. And it's
then that I now believe
  you truly did take a
piece of me with you.

Now, Lord, I need
  your help to
re-invent me? No?

Okay. So, I just
  need to spread my
wings and
  concentrate on
another novel.

And whether I fall
  flat on my face, or
my behind, I 'll get up
  stronger, learn,
pray, and help others,

because you both
believed I could.

P.S Thanks. I just
needed to be
reminded.

"The Ohio Travels of Daniel and Alice"

It was the time of goose
   down pillows and feather
tick mats. Quilts piled high
   o'er three in a bed.

Washboard, lye soap,
   hand-turned wringers,
flat irons steamed to
   spittin' sizzle, atop the

wood-fired range, and
   lye-cracked field corn
hominy. Sweet corn, stir-
   dried, a tasty treat.

Quarts by the hundreds
   lined pantry shelves.
Butter-fat milk, warm
   fresh from Molly.

Catsup on eggs, served
   sunny-side proud.
Wheat, oats, rice,
   cornmeal-mush fried.

Creamy churned butter
   o'er sour dough biscuits
and bread. Smoke-cured
   hams, brown bacon

sides, cracklings, and lard.
  Dried, shelled beans
and ham all-day simmered
  in a tri-legged pot.

Johnny cake, corn bread/
  molasses, spicy bread
pudding. Aprons of spring
  greens, cow slips,

horseradish, dandelion.
  When love was tender,
the winters harsh,
  their one change of

clothes were hand-me-downs.
  High-water pants, scratchy
long johns, line-dried diapers,
  belly-bands and safety pins.

Barefoot innocence. Foot-
  treadled sewing machines.
Kerosene, glowing mantle
  lights, key wound

clocks to chime the hour.
  Man-reined team of
horses guided the sharpened
  plow, from fingers of dawn,

till light of the moon.
   In cap and bibbed over-
hauls, in aproned muslin
   gown. Family ties were

bound by Sunday
   gatherings, perch
by the bushel, from Old
   Woman Creek, that

emptied into Lake Erie and
   meandered through the
William Schatz Farm
   where Don was born.

"My First Bus Tour—The Summer Before 9/11"

The UAW Retirees
  and spouses left
Ohio on a Tuesday for
  A motel in New Jersey.

We took the Ferry
  To Ellis Island
and the Statue of
  Liberty, to later view

New York from the
  Empire State Building,
at night. Earlier we had
  shared a first. A bowl

of sweet potato fries and
  enjoyed the elegance of a
horse and carriage ride
  through Central Park.

Having attended
  several Broadway
musicals in Detroit,
  prepared us

for sitting through
  the impressive
Phantom of the Opera
  at the Majestic Theatre.

However, nothing came
   Close to Reba McIntire
starring in "Annie Get
   Your Gun" at New York's

Marque Theatre. Superb.
   Exciting. Then visited the
lovely St. Patrick's
   Cathedral. Another

surprise. Just inside the
   Church of St. John, a
softly-lit area was posted.
   The Poet's Corner
For American Poets.

We sat in the Gallery
   looking down into the
exciting New York Stock
   Exchange. Buyers

and Sellers called out—
   amounts which
scrolled across the walls
   the day Krispy Kreme

Donuts hit the Stock
   Exchange and brought
to life the enormity of
   having acquired my

Securities License on
   my 70th birthday.

"Midnight"

I just finished Don's family's
  Annual Christmas Newsletter.
The first Christmas in over Sixty years,
  that I signed my name without his.

Habits aren't all that easy to change.
  But every card arrived without his
name, which I'm certain was not
  easy for family and friends either.

He was the last of the aunts and uncles
  of this generation of Starks. But the
generations continue. Great-greats, etc.

and New Years is just a few days away.
I'll be dancing alone this year. Okay it has
  been a few years since we really danced.
But swaying together was still special.

Yes. When he got upset with me and the
  way our lives had changed, limitations
and all, he would say, "Well, when I'm gone
  you can do whatever you want to do."

Now I understand what George meant when
  he used to say—"Being alone is really hard."
But like him, I am trying to take it in stride.
  My sister, Carol said last year at this time,
"You'll soon find, you are a third wheel."

When I'm not writing, I'm watching Hallmark
   about Romance, instead of all sports, but am
following golf on TV. Plus keeping in touch with
   friends and family, enjoying watching my children
and grand-children and great-grandchildren.

   My next novel is hovering—with my
characters chomping at the bit, waiting for me
   to allow my muse free reign in a new mystery.

"Live Your Life"

Live your life
   by filling your days
with memories
   worth remembering
over and over again.

Have no regrets for
   when the loving,
the gentleness, the
   tomorrows that
were never an issue
   were expected—
almost guaranteed!

Yet. How does one
   really prepare?
So unaware how quickly
   life can change. When
the impossible reality
   sweeps in and steals
a huge part of your
   heart, and leaves you
wondering if you were
   ever here.

But wait! That forever
   exists in our children,
our grandchildren,
   greats that follow.

But, I feel so shockingly
  alone and finally
realize what I had taken
  for granted would
always BE—but has
  mysteriously
disappeared like
  a vapor.

Never to return.
  So now; I survive
alone, with
  emptiness tears.

And—Lord, life just
  seems like
make-believe.

Then, I'm reminded
  of the laughter –
the dreams, the
  passion—plus warm
Christmas wishes,
  Christmas dances,
Christmas mornings,
  as they flood my
soul, and I am so
  thankful for all our
magical moments
  together. For, I had
naively thought we
  had forever.

"My Former Destination"

My former
   destination dreams
have been re-routed.

I have had to expand
   my garden of courage
and self-reliance—

bravely fill the silence
   with captivating
songs and acceptance.

This is forever, that
   of dancing alone,
without a partner,

but I can do it with
   memory smiles and
the Lord's support
   and strength.

"For the Last Time"

For the last time
   when one falls in love,
no matter how beautiful
   or handsome, it isn't just
the physical body, but the
   sparkle in their eyes—
their smile, their touch, the
   sensitivity in the electrical
connection of two loving
   spirits—the beating
of two hearts.

But all this ended
   when Don's diseased
worn-out lungs failed
   his heart and…

the last time Don managed
   to exhale, his Spirit
escaped in one loud whoosh
   and disappeared into
the dark of night.

His physical body is
   designated, graciously
identified as military—
   in the space where it
is buried. This his final
   resting place on Earth.

But what of his Spirit?
  That which brought
life to the person we
  had learned to love?
I pray you are now at
  Peace with the Lord.

"Just One More Time"

Honey, I just needed you to
   hug me—just one more time.
I wanted to tell you I love you
   just one more time.
Kiss you good morning, good night,
   just one more time.

But our last goodbye is but
   a memorable whisper,
lingering, yet in cool silence
   impossibly lost

without your physical presence.
   Even the atmosphere is empty.
Your last breath silenced in the
   surreal essence of a heartbeat.

Memories hover…
   surprise me…at odd turns…
sweet reminders of when
   it was…the two of us.

But now, I must pick-up
   the pieces and go on
even midst the love and
   support of strangers
family and friends, but
   must I still stand alone?

No. Allowing God to hold my hand,
   I will make it.
I will be stronger,
   just you wait and see.

The future will have a silver lining,
   with sunshine, smiles and rainbows.
 My heart is stronger now
   for our love is ever with me
as I explore a different universe,
   until we meet again—one more time.

"I'm Doing Okay"

How strange to laugh
   out-loud—all by myself.
It's been awhile.
   The warm, hollow sound
echoed back at me.

Family and friends ask,
   me how I'm doing, and
I reply, "I'm doing okay." I'm
   at a loss to know how a
widow is supposed to be
   doing. But I know they
ask because they care

   and miss him too;
especially sometimes when
   they see me without him;
harder still to stop by the
   house—disappointed
     he is no longer here.

I never dreamed I'd still
   be living in the home
we built and where we
   raised our children.

But it's apparent this step
   towards independent living
isn't all that new, having been

his caregiver for almost three years.
Thank you for asking.
I'm doing Okay.

"Life's Ever Changing Challenges"

Former
   destination dreams-
for-two, have been
   re-organized.

I have expanded
   my garden of
courage and
   self-reliance.

Determined to fill
   the silence with
captivating songs—and
   the ever-changing

dance-of-independence,
   alongside patience,
prayer, and the
   Lord's blessing.

"Milestone Options"

I have been existing in a
   Milestone. Gently removing
parts of the past, but recalling when
   our forever started fading…

months before his spirit/soul
   had reluctantly given up.
When he could no longer
   keep trying, and make believe

became too tiring. But he tried
   to tell anyone who would
listen, when he sang
   'Railway to Heaven'.

Open my heart. Open my eyes.
   Open the blinds. Let in the light.
Face the options. Remove the
   obstacles. Am I existing,

like the trees, as roots deepen,
   branches reaching, sheltering,
shading, existing like a hurricane
   lantern which only lights with

batteries when needed. Timed
   lights set to on—off. Gaining
strength at church on
   a Sunday morning.

But still the hands of time
   keep spinning—not waiting,
but sharpens the blade, as
   decisions echo—move—reach

out, before opportunities
   disappear. Accept yesterday is
gone. Step outside these walls of
   safety? Best woven in silken

memories, etched in stone. Fear step aside!
   This morning's lesson woke me to sunshine.

"Together or Apart"

Although I miss our being together, my
   dance partner, my better half of being
a couple…we were also independent in
   other ways. While he loved bowling,
fishing and golf,
   I love researching, collecting and sharing
family history; pursuing my passion for
   writing. Plus studying and training to keep
my licenses for my financial business up-to-date.

Our differences didn't hurt,
   but enhanced our togetherness.
Thus, I'm not looking for another to
   make my life complete. For, I
doubt getting it right more than once
   is not in the picture.

Six weeks later, however a recent front
   page announcement in the Lima News
headline read, "Lima near top for single
   millennial women" was a shocking surprise.

A dozen family members were gathered at
   The hospital surgery-waiting area when,
a great Nephew announced, "Hey, Aunt
   Marilyn, you made the front page!
Quotes from the Internet and Facebook too!"

My first impression was astonishment. Then
   after reading it, I prayed no one would
take it seriously. I'm several times over and
   past the age of a millennia woman. But
listing me as a famous, published author—
   now that I consider a compliment. However,
a dating service listed me as a single with the
   availability of a great deal of quality men—and
specified my name with two local famous male authors.
   I've only been a widow for four months for heaven's
sake. His clothes are still in his closet, and his
   pillowcase is gathering dust. My, oh my. With this world
of instantaneous data availability; a writer's what-if-ideas
   are endless.

"Sunday Morning"

My arms ache for you today
   cause you're a million miles away
but when you come back to me
   will be the sweetest day—you'll see.

Now I borrow time from yesterday
   when our plans for happiness
lay many months, years ahead
   in our tomorrows.

When I was busy marking time to see,
   paradise was in the loving, you and me.
But now listen honey, while I whisper
   those sweet words you like to hear,

that I can't wait to see you—watch
   your face light up the stars, when our
love shines through our tears, once again
   we'll be touching…loving…holding hands.

"Time Rides the White Stallion"

Published in HM World of Poetry *11-15-1988*
Golden Poet Award 1989

Time rides the white stallion,
   from an embryo of silence to
first breath. Soon first life pierces
   the challenging new world.

Caringly trained to the bit, prances
   proudly, yet determinedly fights
the confining aura to establish its
   unique identity.

Racing the moon towards
   fame's elusive goal,
conquers
   interminable odds.

But while blossoming in
   its isolated galaxy,
blinders blur the warmth
   of the sun.

Then, retiring with resignation and
   spirited syncopation, freely kicks
up its heels, seeking, expanding,
   exploring new ventures—
before forced to clip-clop out
   to pasture.

For, far too soon, time frees the
   White Stallion, as sunsets
misty prism reveals a
   weeping rainbow.

"From Her Favorite Rocking Chair"

The dust had settled
  and revealed
    forgotten memories.
Collections of photos,
  reminders of
    momentous occasions,
inspirations
  challenges,
    scattered dreams.
Blessings and promises
  years of joy, of
    children's footsteps.
Rocking, tears and
  laughter echo
    down the hall.
Listen. Silence stills
  her heart, arms'
    empty, heart full.
Creaking motion
  sings of moments
    when she'd held her
babes at her breast.
  Their trusting eyes
    contented smiles.
Tiny hands that
  clutched and held
    a lock of hair
Or fingers small
  all meshed with

    promises of life—
just beginning a
  future yet unknown.
    Absorbing the love
life offered. Setting
  goals, they grew.
    Left the nest—
challenging their world
  continuing the legacy
    of love and making
their own memories.

"A White Haze"

A white haze hovered ore' the horizon,
   screening the distant woods and farms.
The humidity hovered around 98%. Cool,
   yet muggy, at eight o'clock a.m.

Japanese Ewe shrubs were loaded with red
   buds—like inverted stuffed olives—
or tiny red holly berries. The sun vied
   with the clouds for supremacy.

The small Blue Spruce quivered. The
   fifteen foot tall evergreens swayed
and shivered miniature bronze pine
   cones that lay in clusters—scattered

indiscriminately, top to bottom. The
   staid crabapple tree spread its
branches, angling up—down—under—
   and over. Definitely not a climbing

tree, because of the numerous pointed
   shoots. The Norwegian Maple—solid.
Beautiful in stature and like the young
   willow would be quite easy to climb.

But I don't recall the reason why I was
   looking for Randy and couldn't find him.
Well, I knew he wouldn't try climbing
   the willow again. He had tried it once

when he was five years old. He climbed
   out too far on a branch his own age, it
bent, and slipped out of his hands. He came
   in the house after he claimed to have

hit numerous branches that left bruises
   before he hit the ground. I quit calling
his name, and returned to the kitchen,
   poured a cup of coffee—and looked up

and out of my kitchen window and there
   he was, hiding in a Norwegian Maple
behind our house—with a smile on his face,
   he had found his own quiet space.

My son, Randy had been diagnosed with a Geoblastoma cancerous brain tumor. Even the name is scary. My children took me to a hospital in Ann Arbor, Michigan to see him. Some went to visit him for one-on-one visits, as well.

But this visit was in regard to the possibility of surgery to remove the tumor the size of an egg. A doctor had given permission to pray for Randy. Sean and Randy's wife stayed in his room with me. Unbeknownst to me, my daughters and a grandson were in the waiting room in a prayer circle. Through their phones, they were still supportive while we prayed.

When I opened my eyes, Randy still had his eyes closed—so I finally softly asked, "Are you okay?"

He finally opened his eyes, and with a smile, said, "You slowed down the 'hitch-hiker' (his name for the tumor because it didn't belong there).

The doctor had said I only had a few minutes, and Sean having retired as a nurse, stayed. So I told Sean I would go back to the waiting room. There was a painful grabbing in my stomach, like someone was using a super/duper plunger on it and I just wanted to sit down, but that hallway looked to be never-ending. I felt like I was going to pass out. Earlier I had counted the number of doors between Randy's patient room and the visitor's waiting room.

When I finally arrived at the visitor's room, there were only two people there, my daughter, Christal and grandson Michael. The tears were trapped. I gripped my stomach with both arms as I sat down and Christal got on one knee and kept saying, "Breathe, Mom. Breathe."

It turned out they couldn't do surgery. He went through treatments, but it wouldn't disappear. Now he was home and Hospice would set up soon.

My children had reserved a beautiful three-floored cabin that would sleep fifteen comfortably, in a clearing in front of a woods in upper Michigan for two nights. That way we could either eat there or out in between our visits with Randy.

Previous cabin visitors had been encouraged to write a little something that had happened during their stay. Someone had taken a walk on the cleared path in the woods and had seen a bear.

The first night, we had been seated around a nicely built fire ring—visiting, relaxing, and enjoying the clear sky that was loaded with stars. We named a star after Randy. With several messages from previous visitors, we heard a crashing sound in the woods. We were two car lengths from the cabin, but we raced across the mowed grass to the cabin—gathering cups, bottles, blankets and shoes.

All five of my children have special personalities and agree on many levels, but you know Lord, right now the picture I am getting about my first-born son, Randy, is that prayers are not in the realm of possibly, even a miracle—but that you will soon be hosting a welcome home party for him—and perhaps his Dad will be there to meet him as well? That, apparently, this time the request through prayers is asking a bit too much because this radical, wild, cancerous tumor has gone rogue!

When we first arrived, Randy welcomed us with hand-signals. A thumbs up or down motions that responded to comments. It was apparent talking resulted in too much pain. Of course, others stopped by to visit, and we left for a while and returned with plans to visit the following day, before we needed to head back home. Some of them had to work the following day.

Our Sunday visit was different. I asked Randy if I could put some of my oil across his creased forehead and then asked where else he had pain. He pointed to and barely whispered

"Neck," which was the same side as the tumor, so I spread quite a bit of oil from his jaw down to his shoulder. Sean stayed with him and unexpectedly they had an extensive conversation.

I rushed out of his room and was surprised after I had barely stepped into the nearby bathroom, when I was flooded with both hands full of tissues -- full of tears. It was hard to be quiet.

Just as in the Ann Arbor Hospital—I was once again hit by that painful clutching in my stomach—repeated once again—but I hadn't said a prayer. I just said it might relax him. So, Lord, is it because my unspoken request is beyond the limit? I know you are all powerful! So, does this mean you need him now? In a different way?

Later after he had talked with each of us. Randy knew we were all saying goodbye for the last time. He had an episode after we left.

We attended his funeral the following weekend, and stayed overnight in a different family rental, Randy's siblings, their spouses, and me, their Mom.

Note: When I returned home, I reviewed the notes I had taken while talking to a minister friend. What was I doing wrong? There it was—one of those things he had mentioned two different times. Beforehand pray: "Through me, Lord—Not from Me!"

I have to protect my own health. I am going to have to use this prayer. I had forgotten to use it for my sister when she was in ER at the hospital, one of her lungs had collapsed—a medical team had done a procedure on her and said I could return to her ER room.

When I walked into her room, she was sitting up in the bed, gripping the hand rails, in tears, and begging me to do something. She wanted more pain medication and they weren't prepared to give her anything else.

When they left, I asked her where the pain was and she laid her hand on the spot. She was gripping my left hand in a death-grip and I put some oil on her forehead, and with my right hand on her hand, I prayed. Before I had finished my prayer, her grip on my left loosened to the point of dropping on the bed.

She had dropped back on the bed and had fallen asleep.

Suddenly, the medical team went nuts, saying she had removed the tubes from her back. I said, there was no way. I had been with her the entire time, waiting for one of her daughters to show up so I could go home.

The doctor told them to slap a piece of tape the size of my hand over the incision and hoped they wouldn't have to do the procedure again. After the team left, the doctor said to me, "I know she didn't remove that because I stitched it in."

I sat in the corner of her room, and didn't cry that much, no pain in my stomach. The following day I was diagnosed with Bells Palsy.

"Randy's Funeral"
Read at Randy Stark's funeral August 11, 2018

Randy,
   You were my first baby—
and I am certain—you learned
   your love of music as a
new-born with your Dad holding
   you on his lap—while he
sat at an upright piano and
   played every song in a
fragile discontinued church
   song book, while I sang
along from the kitchen. And
   once in awhile—your Dad
would call out—"I'll bet you
   don't know this one!"
I did.
As a toddler—you would sing
   silly songs when you played
outside. When I couldn't hear
   you anymore—I went looking.

You were six months old when
   we took you on your first
adventure—a road trip to Madison,
   Virginia where your Aunt Alice,
Leonard, and Dean had just moved
   to their new dairy farm. While
there, we toured Thomas Jefferson's
   Monticello near Charlottesville,

Virginia, plus numerous Civil War
  Battlefields.

Practically every grade-school paper
  you brought home became the
first canvas for your art. Years later
  you painted Piglet and Rabbit
from Winnie-the-Pooh, which still
  grace my basement walls.

In high-school, you became the
  first and only Drum Major in
Allen East History. One of your
  claims to fame was playing
Tenor Saxophone as a member
  of 'The 110 Marching Men', of
Ohio University Marching Band,
  when they played in Carnegie
Hall, and had the audience
  dancing in the aisles.

My most embarrassing moment
  was the day you, as a four-year-
old—decided you had worn your
  over-the-ankle high-top shoes
long enough—so while your grandma Edna and I were shopping in
a department store in Lima—
  you spotted a rack of low-cut
shoes—tied in pairs.
  I never noticed this until my mom

and I had our packages in hand,
    and left the store. Then wondering
why you were smiling ear to ear, and
    my mom and the clerk were
laughing at my expression. We
    returned those shoes.

They were the wrong size anyhow,
    but this may have been the start
of allowing you to hand the clerks
    pennies to pay for your choice of
one candy or toy for each of my
    weekly grocery visits.

I've never forgotten the day you
    heard me crying once after
my mom died, and you, as a grown-
    up five year old said, "Don't be
sad mommy. God must have needed
    another Grandma Angel in Heaven
to rock the babies when they cry.

Randy

"We've Named a Star—Randy"

It's not just in the knowing—
   but accepting—that one
of my children is no longer
   on this earth.

I can't call him on the phone and
   Hear him answer, "Hi! Mom."
Or, see his face—the look in his
   eyes when both of us knew—
we were saying goodbye. More
   than once he whispered, "Thank
you for coming. Love you."

And now I must figure out how to
   fill this void with more than
memories—knowing there isn't a
   blessed thing I can do for him now.

Except—to Not Focus on that which
   I cannot change. But—Focus on
those who perhaps, are in need of a
   helping hand—a touch—a smile—
a precious nod—a moment of
   understanding—a prayer.

Our lives really are a two-way street.
   We're busy, either coming or
going. So. May there be miles and
   miles to go, before we complete
Our Dash. God Bless.

I had worked at Superior Coach as the receptionist and personal secretary in the Purchasing Department for at least a year. I loved my job. However, when Don finally found a more stable income, I retired to be a stay-at-home mom.

When his job didn't turn out to be all it appeared to be, I went to work at the First National Bank in Lima's square in the Trust Department. I loved this job as well. Then when Don finally got hired in at Lima's Ford Engine Plant, our Brian was born nine months later.

Shortly after he was born, my mom said, the hat she had crocheted for his big brother would never fit Brian, so she would have to make Brian a hat of his own.

I told my mom that I noticed when Brian was in his high-chair it appeared he was going to be left-handed. Her school-days-memories were very strong regarding anyone being left-handed. (My sister, Susie, always thought she should have been left-handed.) Mom insisted I just needed to put the spoon in his right hand and he would use it.

I decided it would be up to him. He threw a ball with his left hand and soon he picked up the spoon with his left hand. We found other leftie issues when I started looking for left-handed scissors. It was like looking for a needle in a haystack. When he wanted golf clubs, this was another challenge. Except, later his dad made him a beautiful driver for a leftie.

His dad remarked that Brian had the advantage as a

left-handed batter and bowler, as well. Don and I missed seeing him bowl his first perfect game and winning a Lima City Bowling Tournament. But, I don't recall anyone mentioning if being left-handed was-a-plus when being a quarterback in football. Brian was the quarterback for the LaFayette Wolves Midget Football team in the 1969 season when they went undefeated in all Allen County. Their coaches were Jack Rex and Ray Moritz. Brian broke a finger close to the end of the season playoff and Coach Jack said, "You can finish the game. We'll just tape a couple fingers together." So, after the game we had two of our four with a cast on that evening.

Getting back to when Brian was eighteen months old, and his baby sister, Valerie, was born. In those days, a mother was expected to stay in the hospital for five days. Imagine my dismay when I arrived at my mom's—excited about introducing Brian to his new sister.

But, it didn't matter that I had missed him; he didn't remember me. Mom said, "Try laying the baby in the bassinette and then maybe he will come to you." I was heart-broken. Mom went into the kitchen.

I knew he was only eighteen months old and I had been away for five days, so I talked gently to him. Finally. He climbed up on the couch beside me, then scooted onto my lap so I could hug him. It didn't take long before curiosity got the best of him when he heard his baby sister cry.

Several months later, the children were outside playing when I heard Valerie crying. Brian had her by the hand as he walked her to me. Although the tears had ceased, she said, "Brian knocked me down."

Brian's version came soon enough. "She was in the middle of the road and a car was coming so I pushed her into the ditch in front of me."

I swallowed the sick feeling in my stomach and knew I would deal with the what-if aftermath later. "Valerie, you knew you were not allowed to play past the marker in the driveway. So from now on, you will stay in the back yard, or in the house."

Brian, like his brothers and sisters, sang in chorus competitions, solos and swing choir.

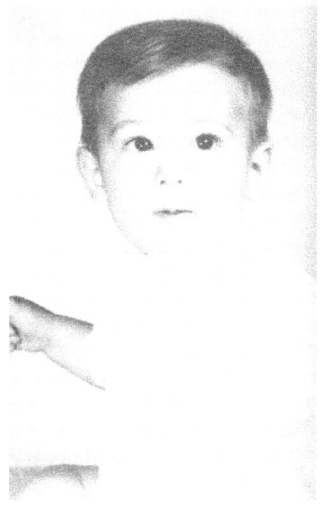

Brian

Valerie was born on Labor Day. My doctor thought my labor had started so I was checked in to a labor room at the hospital early in the morning. My mom's family reunion was the Sunday of Memorial Day weekend, and looking at me when I dropped the boys at her house, she said, "George and I will just take them to the family reunion." She later admitted she didn't think I would have a baby that day anyhow.

For some reason, neither I nor anyone else understood why I started continually rocking gently back and forth in my bed. Every once in a while a nurse would check on me and asked, "Are you in pain? Do you want something for pain?" I always replied, "No," to both questions.

Another asked, "Why are you rocking back and forth?" My reply was, 'I don't know. It just feels good." My doctor almost didn't make it in time for her delivery. It was lunch time after all. My water broke and she was born.

After I was placed into a room, an older nurse stopped in my room and said, 'Well now there's our 'rockin mama'. You rocked her right out. I've never seen anything like it.'

I ironed the ruffles on her outfits. Her hair curled softly. She was a few weeks old, when Don's sister, Altha called to tell me that they were digging the basement for our house in the country.

Valerie was always shy, and wouldn't go to family, much to their dismay. Then one Sunday while casseroles and dishes were being set out for serving, I noticed that her cousin was just sitting there, in a kick-back chair, doing nothing. I walked up to him and said as I handed nine-month-old Valerie to him, "Here. Take her."

Surprised, he hesitated, but before he could shake his head no, she looked at him and smiled. Of course after that—no matter who tried to coax her to come to them, she would turn her head away and hug Gary. He was lost. She had won.

In May 1969, she started lessons in tap dance and ballet in the Patty Spallinger Dance Group. My first thought was why does my shy daughter want to take dance? But she proved us all wrong when their troupe made their first appearance in January 1970, at the Richland Manor Nursing Home.

Years later, Valerie and younger sister Christal were cheerleaders for the Lafayette Midget Football team because their brother, Brian, was playing. A broken arm didn't stop her cheering in green and white, cast and all. Plus their dad was one of the four LaFayette Midget Football Referees from LaFayette.

Valerie's first year in sewing in 4-H, I received a phone call requesting if there were any girls who might be interested in doing a demonstration at the Ohio State Fair. No one was free due to vacations or other projects. Valerie made up a poster using a Barbie doll pattern to describe how to place a pattern on fabric properly before cutting.

Valerie was waiting her turn to do her demonstration while the girl ahead of her was frying chicken in an electric skillet. The chicken was sizzling while this girl was describing each step. She was rudely interrupted when a rooster crowed, "cock-a-doodle-do", from the far side of the huge theatre.

Smiles and chuckles rippled from the crowd to the parents and other contestants to the 4-H Judges. Tension eased and the demonstrators were more relaxed just in time for Valerie's demonstration.

Valerie

How Writing Changed My Life

❦

The day Christal was born, the sun was shining and I knew at some time she was certain to be in some sort of activity because whenever I moved, she moved before she was born, she didn't just kick or punch me, she did cheers.

However while I was in the delivery room before she was born, I overheard nurses talking about a woman in the other delivery room had had another boy and this woman already had a girl, and I heard something about switching babies?

After she was born I heard a baby crying and when I asked if that was my baby across the room, they said, "Yes." I asked if she could be beside me, and they agreed. They laid her beside me and the moment she heard my voice, she stopped crying. With my arm around her, the two of us were wheeled out of the delivery room together.

When she was a toddler she and her dad's Weimaraner hunting dog, Duke, became friends.

When she was outside playing, I watched her from inside. Sure enough, within seconds, whenever she wandered too close to the road, Duke had a certain bark that let me know she had wandered too far.

Christal was the youngest at this time which meant whenever we had plans to go away, I dressed her last and sure enough while I dressed, she had to rush outside to hug Duke goodbye. He licked her face and she smelled like dog.

I was busy at my sewing machine in those days, but I refused to make jeans. However she challenged me the day she came home from school on a weeknight and said, "Mom I made Homecoming Queen. I need a new outfit by next Friday night." We went to the mall shopping and she found a pattern and the fabric she liked for a matching skirt and vest, in a wool blend plaid. Another time she needed a dress that would make her look younger for the musical, Sound of Music. She was also in Chorus and Swing Choir.

Christal played drums in Allen East Jr. High and High School Band.

Christal and Valerie joined 4-H and I was asked to take over as the LaFayette Boys and Girls Advisor until someone decided it was too upsetting for all the children to not receive a blue ribbon. A blue ribbon had always been granted to children when they finished their first year project.

However, when it was extended to anyone for any project, my daughters and I quit 4-H after that. My daughters said if they followed directions and worked hard, there was a chance to earn a blue ribbon. If not, they would try for one the next year.

I once thought the year I made Raggedy Ann and Andy dolls for Christmas was my biggest challenge – mainly because my sewing machine was in the kitchen, I could only sew while they were in school.

However, the largest sewing project was Christal's wedding. Ever since she was a little girl, she had said that Mom was going to make her wedding dress, but when the time came she surprised me by asking me if I would. She designed what she wanted: one pattern for the basic dress, another pattern for the neckline and another one for the sleeves. But she was going to make her hat. Plus the fabric store ordered a bolt of fabric from New York for the attendants' dresses from a size two to a size sixteen.

I was at one of Christal's games, when a gentleman from an opposing team told me which girl was his daughter and asked, "Do you have a family member playing? "Yes," I replied, and gave him her number. "But she's a blonde. Does she bleach her hair?"

"No. She is a brown-eyed natural blonde. Her dad was a blonde. Her brown eyes she gets from her mom. Me," I replied.

Christal loved sports. She played in a summer softball league. Allen East High School Volleyball and Basketball. An Allen East high school administrator told me he thought Christal was the first woman in the school to receive a scholarship for college in sports. She had received an offer from Adrian College in volleyball but turned it down. She tried out at Northwestern Business College and they paid her schooling for playing the season in basketball.

Years later, after marriage and while raising two sons, she coached Allen East Junior High and High School volleyball. Her sister Valerie became a high school volleyball referee during this period.

Christal

Sean was born in the spring when we lived in the country. He weighed almost nine pounds. The only mishap before he was born was that I had left Christal with my niece, Judy, while I drove in to see my ObGyn.

When I returned to pick up Christal, I slipped and lost my balance walking down hill on wet grass. I flipped over on my tummy and couldn't get up. I was like an upside-down turtle. My hands and feet barely touched the ground, however I couldn't get up without Judy's help.

Even after she helped me inside her home, I was still frightened that I might have hurt my baby and called my doctor. He asked how I was. I replied that I was fine as I struggled with tears that I was afraid I had hurt the baby. "You're okay. Good. Your baby is well protected and will be fine."

From the day he was born, anytime Don stopped in at the hospital for a visit, Sean was more attentive when he heard his dad's voice. That continued after we went home. He could be playing in the playpen and let it be known that he wanted his dad to pick him up when he came in the room.

Sean had been walking around furniture at ten months and anytime the organ was turned on he was singing. Move forward and one day in kindergarten his teacher had tired of Sean talking to another student and said if he didn't quit talking, he was going to have to come to the front of the class and talk.

He went to the front of the classroom and asked if he

could sing instead. She agreed and he sang a song his dad had taught him, "Ice Cream Cone". His teacher enjoyed it so much she left the classroom and returned with the music teacher who asked him to sing it a second time, and sang in a quartet in an Allen East High School Musical, Music Man.

He played coronet in Allen East Jr. High and High School Band. He said once when he was waiting his time to play his coronet in District Competition that he would rather sing than play.

Years later as a senior, he sang "Surfing U.S.A." while riding a skateboard. He was also in Allen East Chorus and Swing Choir, and sang with seniors in the district under the direction of a music teacher from Bowling Green State University, as they performed in Lima's Civic Center. He said the acoustics were so fantastic that he could not only hear the student behind him, but the person on his right, left, all around him.

At the age of five, Sean went fishing for Carp in Riley Creek with his dad using cornmeal dough balls I had cooked in a pan that was one-step from being used for peelings on their way to the compost pile. The Carp he snagged weighed so much, he had to have help bringing it in. Later when they brought it home, someone had to help hold it up so we could get a picture. The Carp was as long as he was tall.

He was always challenging me in his own way. This was about the time when standing in front of a full length mirror, he asked me how many hearts he had. I replied, "You have only one heart." His next question was, "Then why can I feel my heart beating here and here and here."

He had pointed out his heart, wrists, and his temple. I hunted through my encyclopedia and found a picture of where his one heart was located.

He became a male nurse, but years later changed careers.

Sean

Don was the youngest of his eight sisters and two brothers. By the time I met him, he had graduated high school and just returned from having served in the Army in Korea and Japan.

Thus sooner or later, I met those who lived in the area more often than the three who lived in a northern county, about ninety minutes away. The first summer after we met, several of his family were visiting and wanted to visit their sister, Altha who lived a few miles away.

But the only vehicle available was Don's 1939? Plymouth. However it was a stick-shift and not one of them wanted to drive it because getting it into second was tricky. So they asked, "Marilyn, do you know how to drive Don's car?"

I admitted I could. Of course they teased me when I shifted it into second as smooth as silk. With my open hand on top of the gear, I shoved it up with a little dip down just bit – then way up, and with my hand under the gear I drew it back towards me into third.

Years later, the summer after their Mom died, a few of his sisters decided they wanted to put flowers on their parents' graves, but couldn't decide which one of them would drive. Their husbands decided I should drive them. After all, it was a ninety minute drive just to Norwalk where they decided to eat lunch, and another half hour to the cemetery.

I still wish I had recorded them. They talked and laughed the entire time. They were so excited – free to share childhood memories. The atmosphere was filled with love and respect.

I had no idea this trip would be so special when the families made their plans and I was asked to drive. Thus my passengers were Altha, Linnie, Dorothy and possibly Cynthia from the Lima area. We were meeting up with Alice, Juanita, and maybe Gladys who planned to meet us at the restaurant on Main in Norwalk. Even the waitresses enjoyed this sisters' party.

Usually when they got together to play cards, visiting was kept at a minimum, which made today very different. Today they were just reminiscing and sharing, and backseat driving when I took a different route, until I reminded them that I had attended school in this area. No I was not lost.

When they played Euchre, it was play cards or take care of your children. No interruptions. Which was why I seldom played. But I played when there were just a few, or to fill out a set.

I played cards at Juanita's when we spent weekends at their farm. I was just starting Don's family history, and Juanita knew where all the cemeteries were in the Huron, Erie Counties and was a big help when we were tromping through cemeteries.

After we ate and were preparing to leave the restaurant, the waitresses almost didn't get their tips. The waitress noticed I had only ate half of my meal and asked if I wanted a 'doggie bag', and I said, "Yes. Thank you."

Dorothy's comment was, "Marilyn, you don't have a dog." Smiles and soft chuckles followed as we gathered our purses and jackets. Dorothy rushed up to us with our tips in her hand. "You guys left money on the table." One of the girls went back and took care that the waitresses got their tips, followed with hugs and explanations as to how things had changed.

I had cemetery notes, from a previous funeral regarding where the road forked to the right and to the left. The name of the cemetery road we wanted had been changed. But that didn't bother this group. More than one said, we always take the one to our right.

"Acceptance? Never!"

Accept it! Give up! Relax!
    But she refuses as her
body and mind deteriorates
    with age and disease.

In gleams of consciousness
    she has no future, no hope,
no release, yet smiles when
    pages of miniscule memories
    flash through the window in
her mind, soothing, yet fading
    like a broken neon sign.

Cooling breezes whispering through Ohio Maple, Oak and Pine,
    through screened second floor farmhouse windows and shears.
Her hands warming, sifting through scoops of warm garden soil,
    the taste of plump strawberries, tomatoes, and raspberries red.

The heady fragrance of Mock Orange, Peony, and Rose.
    Waking to morning birdsong and the competitive
crowing of Banty roosters, Jake and Ned.

Of moonlit evenings, back porch talk, Prince Albert pipe-smoke,
    calico kittens swatting at elusive fireflies,
English blue tick coon hound dogs treeing a raccoon.
    Memories of yesterday's childhood capers with family and friends
remain encapsulated—elusive—keeping her forever young.

Trapped. With no escape.
   Once again, she fights the
restraints that stifle her freedom,
     her independence.

Her hands flutter out of sync. Her
     feet tremble in useless anticipation.
Frustration erupts in volcanic keening.
     Accept it? Never!

The Celebration Of Russel G's Life
Read at his funeral, May 21, 2018

The first time I met Russel was in January
   1954. I had just got off work at the Big
Wedge on Findlay Road in Lima, and was
   waiting for Jack to arrive to introduce

me to his best friend, Don, who had just
   returned home from Korea. Russ was
Don's nephew. Russ was also married
   to Jack's sister. They were family.

Several months earlier, Jack's fiancé, Pat
   and I had become friends while riding
the city bus. She was on her way to the
   attorney's office where she worked, and

I was just starting classes at Northwestern
   School of Commerce on East High Street
just off North Main Street. It was awhile
   before I even knew Russ wore a leg brace

to support his one leg weakened by polio.
   He was tough as nails! With a heart of Gold!
In addition to working a full-time job and
   raising a family, he didn't hesitate to tramp

over snow-covered fields on Thanksgiving
   day, hunting rabbit and pheasant with family.
He and Nola enjoyed the peaceful, quiet past-
   time of fishing. He and Don coached Lafayette

Boys' Pee-Wee summer league baseball and
 was involved in organizing the LaFayette Girls'
summer league softball. And Yes. He also was a
 dyed-in-the-wool 'Detroit Tigers' fan.

Russ went to Columbus to fight for a law that
 required ramp-access to public buildings.
He knew from personal experience, he had
 lost track of the number of times

he couldn't enter businesses and homes
 of family members. His love of history,
beside reading about it, he traveled to and visited
 the capitals of each of the fifty states in the U.S.A.

He enjoyed visiting family and friends—fascinating
 us all with his impeccable memory. When he first
acquired his first battery-powered transport chair, he
 challenged mobility safety rules, by getting dumped

a time or two. He was even warned by a Florida Mall
 Security Guard to slow down; as Nola raced to keep
up with him, and Don and I ran to catch up with Nola.
 He enjoyed music, especially recordings of Jazz, and

movies on the Big Screen. Don & I got a taste of Broadway
 Musical Productions with them, in several Detroit
Theatres. However one memorable evening, after an
 enjoyably meal with friends, Don was dancing with Nola,

and Russ and I were sitting alone at the table – when he remarked softly, "I wish I could dance with her like that." Perhaps now he can. He was also active in quite a few organizations over the years before he retired.

"Remembering Nola"
Read at Nola's funeral

Well known, for her compassionate nature,
   She danced, played cards and the slots—often
proudly bragging about her family and friends.

Fun trips with Russel at the wheel and Harold as
   co-pilot, with Nola and Nadine in the back seat;
listening to music and singing—with just-a-bit of
   humorous back-seat driving advice.
Don and I were following in our car.

We visited: New York's Baseball Hall of Fame,
   stopped in Boston, and filmed October's
fall colors and history in the New England states.
   Plus, whale watching on the windy Atlantic Ocean.

   **Please keep in mind these road trips were
   BEFORE cell phones & GPS—Walkie-talkies!**

A week at Coldwater Lake, Michigan; Nola, Russ,
   Nadine, Harold, and Don went out daily after
a sunrise breakfast—to fish off the Pontoon Boat
   her brother, Jack was navigating.
Ann and I enjoyed shopping and cooking
   on the challenging black iron, gas stove that
had to be as old as our grandparents.

Early on, Nola & Russ had introduced us to Broadway
   in Detroit's theatres. She especially loved musicals.

Seated a few steps from stage left, her eyes were
  sparkling because she knew the words to every song.

Nola's love of flowers were in abundance in
  Hawaii, which began with our arrival greeting:
Aloha, plus a lei of orchids was promptly placed
  around her neck. Orchids, Plumeria and Red
Hibiscus were just a few of her favorites.

With permission through the stewardess, our
  return trip home was Highlighted when we
climbed a ladder in the 747 to talk to the pilot.

We visited: Elvis Presley's Graceland and historic Mud
  Island Park along the Mississippi in Memphis, TN.
Further on, to an Indian Rodeo at Window Rock, AZ.

Breathtaking, Canyon de Chelle National Monument,
  (Navaho Nation) Arizona. Watched artist, Calvin Thomas,
(ANAZASI (Puebloan) paint Ink-Art on a piece of Sandstone.
  The following morning, we learned of 911, at breakfast in
Gallop, New Mexico and were forced to stay an extra night
  in Phoenix, Arizona—until the travel ban was lifted at
Boulder Dam. Plane travel was still grounded several days
  after our arrival in Las Vegas.

A Texas Champion Rodeo in Mesquite, The Riverwalk in San
  Antonio, The Alamo, Padre Island, The Stark Museum of Art
in Orange, Texas, which featured a Bronze Remington
  sculpture in the foyer. No wonder a Pinkerton man followed
us from room to room.

We walked across the Rio Grande Bridge through Customs
 into Mexico, from the border-town of Brownsville, Texas,
where Love Birds flew in every night to roost.

Avery Island, Louisiana Jungle Garden is the only place
 where TABASCO sauce is made, and where Nola walked out
on a narrow strip of land—trying to coax a baby alligator to
 surface. Thankfully, not one—was curious enough to
respond to her enticing sweet-talking.

Double-parked on a busy street in the pouring rain, in
 New Orleans. Cajun music drifted out into the street—while
Nola dashed into a shop to purchase a Christmas -Tree ornament
 to add to her collection. Rain had set-in for the day,
thus we toured inside The Aquarium of the America's.
 The main feature was TWO—huge, blue-eyed, Albino
Alligators, just lying there in a glass cage.

After Sunset in the Florida Keys, Orlando, Tampa, Clearwater,
 The Villages; we then sailed out of the Sponge Docks at Tarpon
Springs for elbow-to-elbow, Deep Sea Fishing.
 Nola's favorite Pelicans were perched on the piers, waiting for
the boats to return.

"Harold's Legacy"
Read at Harold's Funeral

Harold's Legacy—was sharing
  the joy of eighty years of
living life to the fullest—
  whether as the loving

caretaker of his family—
  traveling cross-country…
to simply sitting on the front
  porch of the house he built,

watching the birds battle over
  the feeders—to the satisfaction
of plowing a straight furrow,
  then proudly harvesting

buckets of strawberries, and
  tomatoes for Nadine to
preserve, plus sharing with
  family and friends.

Remembering that quirky
  'gotcha' smile when he
trumped his opponents Ace?
  Because he loved winning!

With his armchair antics and
  coaching—The Ohio State
Buckeyes, The Oklahoma Sooners,
  or The Cleveland Browns

should never have lost a game!
  But, his greatest legacy is
continuing his love of family, and
    their cherished memories of him.

"Remembering Nadine"

As a child, singing was as
natural as breathing. Her Dad,
George would not condone
fighting in the car, and lucky

for her mom and dad, their
five children: Nadine, Nola,
Jack, Jim, and Carol, harmonized
beautifully. They handed down

their love of music and singing
to following generations.
Nadine's heart and home was
usually filled with music,

especially Elvis Presley's albums
and movies. Like music, she
also loved her favorite teams: the
Cleveland Indians and Ohio

State, except, of course, any game
or antic involving her children,
grandchildren or great-grandchildren.
They were always subjects of

conversation. Many times they took
precedence over playing cards—
and she thoroughly enjoyed playing
cards. Numerous weekends, they

visited Harold's sister, Juanita and
   her husband at their farm near
Norwalk, Ohio and his sister, Alice
   and family's dairy farm in the

mountains near Culpepper, Virginia—
   and later picking oranges and grape-
fruit in Alice's Florida backyard.
   Nadine kept detailed journals of

their cross-country vacations and
   their in-the-trunk-of-the-car picnics.
As their children grew up, Nadine
   and Harold vacation-traveled cross-

country with siblings and their spouses.
   Don and I joined them on some of
these travels, from one coast to the other.
   She was a vegetarian, yet she cooked

the fish, the pheasant, the squirrel, and
   whatever else her 'hunters' proudly
brought home, even though she wouldn't
   eat anything with feathers or fins.
Now that's love!

"Song Of Farewell"
Written about JoAnn for Jim Condon

Now I am no longer in pain
   but rest, knowing my 37 years
were not in vain,

for great was the life and love
   i shared with you,
which lives on in our
   sons numbering two,

plus a lifetime of memories
   shared with loving family
and friends—old and new.

   When the minister began,
      "Ashes to Ashes—Dust to Dust,"
A song-bird settled in a nearby
seedling *tree. It's song plaintive—*
   haunting.

"We return from whence we came,"
he continued. "We pray for loved
   ones left behind. Amen."
      Birdsong filled the uncomfortable silence.

"This concludes our service," he added.
      Birdsong held the attendees motionless.

When the minister added, "You may return to your cars."
> *The songbird flew out of sight.*

> *I sang my song of Farewell,*
> *To you,   to you,   to you.*

"Unexpected Adieu"

We'll remember Gene's Mary
   with the smiling face—
her soft spoken
   voice lingers in
     our hearts.

It didn't seem it
   should be her time
to leave her earthly
   home, her family
     and her friends.

But then—time is
   not ours to plan
and mold. If you
   didn't get the chance

to say goodbye before,
   God knows,
Mary knew we cared,
   and merge our

prayers and thoughts
   In lovingly
bidding her an
   unexpected
Adieu in April 1992.

"A Visit with my Aunt Lou"

A visit with my Aunt Lou
who lived alone in her
Penthouse apartment, surrounded
  by her collection of'
    memories and photos.
Some made her chuckle—
  others challenged heart ache,
yet she couldn't let go of the past.

She said, "I can't. It's all I have."
  She defended righteous paybacks
guilt-sandwiched between
  right and wrong,
trapped in yesterday
  as pain restricted, and meds
clouded what could have been.

As sorrow clung—tears fell—
  for she was caught in a time-warp
of her making, her comfort zone.

Then her memory flipped into reverse
  as topics tumbled and bumped into
the local news events. Reminders of
  another time brought a misting
of tears that dampened her face.

Still beautiful and cocky. Then
  pride flashed in her tired, dark eyes.

Her voice raised, upset about what
  she had once had, and lost.
She needed a cane to support her
  broken, bent, repaired body.
Alone, and lovely midst her
  memories, regrets and roses.

Arthritis had stilled the strings of her guitar.
  Time rusted her lovely songs.
Still her crooked fingers momentarily
  danced across the polished piano keys.
But forgiveness was still the stranger
  which separated her from her loved ones,
for she firmly believed, the past was all she had.

"Aunt Marjorie, Goodbye at Ninety-Eight"

My childhood memories included riding with you
   and Uncle Harley in his coupe that you said you
painted while he was in the military. I rode with the
   two of you, and he asked me if I had ever eaten

pickled pig's feet. 'You haven't lived till you've tried
   them.' I don't recall ever trying them, and put them
in George's category of oddities: he loved breaded
   chicken's feet and breaded pumpkin blossoms.

But I prefer your homemade Apple Butter and whatever
   pie you take a notion to bake. I loved listening to your
charming memorable stories about the family. You always
   knew the answers. You are a great storyteller, and you

never knew a stranger, because by the time they heard a story
   about how life was when you were growing up, you
had just made a new friend. I knew your favorite place to
   shop was at Goodwill. You could look at most anything

past-its-prime and look like new again with brush strokes of
   paint. Make it your style with a stitch or two on her sewing
machine. Buying an organ for five dollars, you were certain it
   would fit in Mike's car. You cleaned it, gathered your music

and although it had been years since you'd played, smiling you
   were soon playing sweet music at ninety-five years young. You
and your son, Mike attended Don's and my 60th
   Wedding anniversary. Our family fascinated with the way you

entertained them. Her funeral later, at age ninety-eight.

Marjorie, spouse of Harley, mother of Mike, Steve, Emily and Diana, will be fondly remembered as family historian, former church
organist, storyteller, seamstress, artist and kitchen recipes magician in the family. She will be greatly missed.

WHITE

"Words in Motion"
First Place LAWC Poetry Contest 2003

Poetry is words in motion
   gathered together
to paint word pictures
   in our minds,
      in our hearts,
         and in our dreams.
Words dance across the page
   searching for their rhythm – their rhyme,
      their sequence in time.
Authors entice us to turn the page
   to follow and feel,
      become part of their story,
         laugh, cry tears,
            learn a lesson—be it any age.
Colorfully bound tomes
   shelved side by side
express authors'
   cherished memories,
      historical happenings—
         incredible imagination.
Turn a phrase here,
Turn a phrase there.
      To survive, authors must
         trust the muse—
            and allow it free reign.
But use words with caution,
   with care—and remember,
      words can also cut like a knife
         and break most any heart.

Read on—and on—and on,
   in any language—
engraved on paper—in granite, or stone,
         on leather, plastic, silver or gold.
    Cherished words in motion
       continue to inspire
           actors, musicians, and authors alike
            in the fulfillment
                of their dreams.

"Boulevard"

A boulevard
   Is a street
divided by a
   grassy strip of
landscaped
   serenity,

of man using
   nature as a
relaxing oasis
   between
destinations.

Woodlawn is
   appreciated as
a beautiful historic
   reminder of
 some of Lima's
affluent founders.

"Family Christmas Celebration"

The Christmas Tree,
   the symbol of life,
once-a-year dangles
   baubles of blue and
     silver memories.

Linking braches of prickly
   feelings with winking
strands of hesitant boisterous
   red, soft welcoming pink,

subdued cautious amber,
   exotic dependable blue,
flirtatious challenging green.

Nostalgia blends with the
   fragrance of pine.
A hushed excitement waltzes
   midst crystalline and tinsel.

As unspoken realities hum hosts
   of carols—haunts shadows of
forgotten images and
   gaily wrapped surprises,

proclaims peace with the
   flight of the dove,
the wings of an angel, the
   flickering of a candle,

  and satisfied sighs.
    All anticipating
      ringing the bells for
        yet another New Year.

"Fourth of July Conversation"

The Bellevue Gazette had written,
  author of "The Flutist and The
Dancer", Marilyn R. Stark, will be
  at the Flat Rock Church near the
children's home, for a book-signing,
  after the Flat Rock annual Fourth-
of- July- Parade.

"Hello," greeted a deep-voiced tall
  stranger dressed in Policeman's blue.
"I volunteered for traffic control for
  today's Flat Rock 4th of July Parade,

when I read you were planning to be here
  today. May I have a word with you?" he
added, as he approached me amid the
  throng of people.

"I came to tell you my story." His compelling
  eyes shimmered with emotion. "I knew
you would understand. My Mother died
  when I was a baby. Foster homes were

found for seven of us. It took my siblings
  longer to find me, because when I was
adopted, my name was changed. I was
  twenty-eight years old when my siblings
suddenly revealed I wasn't an only child.

I have brothers, sisters, nephews, nieces,
   etc., but I feel this haunting, missing
connection that is hard to wrap my
   head around. They're nice people

understand. A friendly group. But we're
   missing shared remembrances,
that of touching, caring, loving,
   laughing, fighting, life in general…"

His voice softened, "Because,
   of this family separation, I am left
with so much empty space,
   here in my heart"… a longing
for what we never shared.
   Like walking into the wrong family
reunion. I did that once."

"Didn't they want to know what
   your adoptive parents were like?"
I asked. "Just the fact that your
   older siblings have searched for
you all these years is pretty special.

"Instead of what you've missed,
   perhaps over time, you can fill
that empty space with what you
   have gained.

"Have you had the chance to find out what their interests or hobbies are? Or are you still in the mode of just remembering their names?" I teased.

He smiled. "Thank you for your understanding smile and suggestions. You are easy to talk to. I wish you well with your writing," he added, and nodded as he warmly shook my hand.

A Handkerchief?

What has happened to the
   handkerchief? Once dainty,
colorfully, framed in crochet
   and lace for a sneeze

now and then or found
   folded in a birthday card.
Men's plain white however
   were twice the size and fit

nicely in their hip pockets,
   or in sturdy country red
which were as essential as
   wearing socks. However-

the red kerchief was more
   likely to be used to wipe
moisture from ones' brow
   or wrapped around the neck.

But more recently they
   became last minute masks
to help control the spread of
   the Covid 19 Virus. Imagine!

Even though I had my shots and
   wore a mask, my doctor ordered
I get tested. I had this dastardly
   Virus twice and didn't know it!

"A Lady Revealed"

Contemplating my 1800's
   kitchen cupboard, engraved
Stanley USA, purchased from
   perhaps Sears or Montgomery

Ward, makes me wonder what
   recipes, secrets, memories you
could share from over the years.
   Your body was built of solid

white oak and sealed with
   a gray waxy 'milk-paint' and
topped first in white paint
   with stickers of kitchen tools.

I stripped, and sanded off
   multiple coats of white, yellow,
turquoise, blue, pink ,barn-red,
   and white again and in between.

Sanded to the natural wood grain,
   she sports shiny metal hinges,
latches, knobs and is proudly
   displayed in a space of her own.

Open doors reveal shelves for cups,
   dishes, glasses, bakeware, a
cookbook or two hidden behind the
   slide-to-the-side rolling doors, a
hanging flour bin, tins for lard, salt,

sugar, tea, coffee, and spices. The
white enamel pull-out counter is
   the center for rolling and cutting

biscuits, noodles, pie dough, cookies
   and bread. Beneath the counter, are
drawers for utensils plus a tin
   bread and pastry drawer.

Space for pots, pans and crocks.
   She stands on tapered solid wood
legs, heeled with metal caps, and
   black rubber casters. Today proudly
displays a clock to mark the time, tools,
   cards, books, dolls, collectibles.

No. She's not perfect. My mom
   needed more shelf space,
thus the flour sifter was removed.
   This cupboard was replaced
when my Mom's new cupboards
   were built, but this lady was
still admired, respected, had a
   new life in the offing.

May I, in my imperfections, also
   be remembered with love and
respect, changing with time, to
   cherish family memories that
continue to grow generation
   after generation.

"A Million Years Ago? I Wonder…"
Honorable Mention in 2000 LAWC Poetry Contest

I wonder…
   what people thought
     a million years ago…
   when they looked at the stars, the moon
     the birds, lakes, rivers, trees, fauna, and
   felt the warmth of the sun, the chill of snow.

I wonder…
   how they dealt with loneliness, peace,
     fear, destruction of their enemies,
   their friends, lovers, their children, and
     pressures beyond their control.

Today…
   opportunities, communication – even
     millisecond cyberspace technology cannot duplicate
   the wonder of trust, emotional space, and time.

I wonder…
   who will read the words I have written,
     find the serenity I have found,
     walk the paths I have walked,
     harvest the perennials I have planted
     enjoy similar pleasant summer afternoon breezes
       scented with honeysuckle, rose and pine.

I wonder...
   will my silent contemplation and laughter drift
     like a reticent muse through the windows
  and walls of the house I call home,
    long after I am gone?
     I wonder...

"White Elephant"

A white elephant
  with his trumpet
in the air.

Is a symbol of
  good wishes
and good luck.

When you believe
  in rainbows
and tomorrow

prosperity will
  shine on you
once again.

And then ...
  with loving care
just pass it on.

"An Artist's Palette of Ohio's Fall"

October's leaves circle and
  drift onto pristine
    green persimmon,
Sprinkled with
  caramel, and cream.
    Trimmed in
strawberry and plum.
  Topped with frost
    and lime.
Painted leaves blanket
  edges of the fairway
    as candlelight captures
    apple and apricot.
God's majestic pastels
  brush hillsides
    and valleys in a
continuous mix of
  perky pumpkin,
    silent cinnamon
and wild cherry
  which are alive with
    vibrant wine
cocky copper and
  robust rust.
    Tantalizing tangerine,
streaks startling scarlet
  on provocative peach
    succulent strawberry
and groovy green.

Luscious lemon glows
   glorious gold, beside
persistent grape and
   memorable melon in
      flamboyant bouquets.
Cotton candy swirls
   brush strokes
      displayed on Poplar,
Buckeye, Maple, Elm
   Hickory, Walnut, Oak
      Ash and Cottonwood.

"Artificial Intelligence"

This term was coined by John
 McCarthy in 1956 at the
Institute of Technology.
 "Artificial Intelligence is the
branch of computer science
 concerned with making
computers behave like people."

Regarding Al's Robot—built with
 an electronic Brain, void of
content, lacking substance—this
 empty vessel is without emotion,
love or caring. Devoid of warmth,
 expression, not a trifle bit of
feeling sympathy, perceive,
 comprehend, or understand
peoples' individual personalities.

Data Science Academia for 2016
 Service Assistant feeds condensed
information to a human symbiotic
 Robot that can walk and talk with
People—is a cloud-based IT infra-
 structure platform that serves as
a Remote Brain which bridges between
 The Real and the Virtual World.

Imagine walking through fragrant
   enclosed Elizabethan Gardens of
Shakespeare's Home in Stratford-
   Upon-Avon.
Stand before the Mona Lisa at
   The Grand Louvre in Paris.

Be surrounded in silent anticipation at
   Mallory Square in Key West, as the
Sun disappears beyond the Horizon of
   The Gulf of Mexico. Meanwhile, layers
of gray swiftly steal the daylight—as
   twilight chills your skin.

"Beginning Again"

Why people downsize
   results in new beginnings—
when loss of a job or promotion
   forces them to re-locate. And
if their parents wish to be a
   part of their lives & grandchildren's
lives—they follow. And, if the
   parents move, for whatever
reason—the family follows.

Retirees downsize their homes,
   their friends, their lifestyle,
as though patterned.
   Assumptions were the norm—
not always a choice. Like stepping-
   stones in reverse, to shed a
lifetime of memorabilia, or to start
   over—with less obligations.

Move to warmer climates.
   Travel the world. Or simply
turn off the freeway and
   cruise down the boulevard.

"Cherished Memories Collections"

It amazes me how
   families die—and
their cherished collections
   disappear. But their

names may appear in a
   cemetery, obituary,
cremated, and even that
   can disappear on a

breeze, like they never
   existed. Unless children,
aunts, uncles, cousins,
   friends share photos
     for when memories fade.

What remembrance crowds-in
   on your thoughts
reflecting on your D-A-S-H?
   (the space between your date
of birth and date of death.)

"Cooling Thoughts To Mow By"

Off to the west
  the darkened sky
looked menacing, but
  the grass needed cut.

Time was of the
  essence in the
breath-stealing
  ninety-degree heat.

Plus, I was fighting-off
  a very determined
deer-fly; expecting
  lunch, like last week.

No doubt, as it
  dove at me—
time and time again,
  abruptly turning

away from the Skin-
  so-soft oil I
had spread on my
  skin. I smiled, and

continued mowing
  back and forth across
the lawn, repeating

these cooling words:
a quirky, cute, curly,
  crooked, cucumber
from Quebec, kept my
  mind chillingly

distracted as I
  finished mowing
the lawn shortly before
  the icy hail and rain.

"Dear Erika"

A new date to remember
   first week in July 1980.
Yes, your name added -
   makes my calendar bright.

We welcomed your arrival,
   spread the news far and wide.
Born at 4:16 a.m. on a Monday
   you started the week out just right.

Tipping the scales at 7 lb.4oz.
   measured in inches, 19-1/2.
A beautiful blue-eyed bundle,
   precious, lively and tanned.

Now your dark hair
   doesn't fool us for a moment,
for your lashes and brows
   are quite blond.

You are loved close-at-home
   Pontiac, Michigan I am told
and afar near Lima, Ohio.

No. The distance in miles
   will not change or diminish
the love in our hearts
   we'll continually send.

"Detroit's Auto Jewels"

2008-2009, A sign of the times,
  No Happy Holidays Here…

Once, acres of ready-for-sale
  4-wheeled, polished jewels
parked in this stop-over
  between factory and show-room.

Now, abandoned acres
  lie barren—except for a few
gutsy, parched weeds framing
  deserted concrete squares.

"Disney World—Epcot—Mgm"

Disney assaults all your senses:
  your sense of vision,
smell, taste, adventure,
  and takes you to
the realm of the past
  and the future,
from the time of creation
  when dinosaurs ruled,
thumping across the land,
  fighting and roaring;
allowing you to see yourself
  as charging your opponent
or just sitting by in placid
  acceptance; to reaching,
soaring to the stars—the galaxy—
  surrounding you with music
and animation.

Tugging
  swirling the heart with whimsy,
with joy and color, with
  shapes that tantalize;
lights and speed that surprise,
  confuse and enlighten.

Nonsense that makes light of
  your insecurities, yet assures,
informs, answers questions before
  the awareness if that need is
apparent and then, presents
  unconscious thoughts into
    acceptable form.

Then, allows you to observe
   and become a part of the
mystery, the enchantment of
   make-believe; from the writers
and artists to the silver screen.

You feel a part of sets that aren't
what they seem; but through
   engineered computers, flames whoosh,
swords zoom, mountains of water
   thunder, yet only mist the
unsuspecting. Then instructs, as you
   absorb the realm of backstage:
from the green room, in costume
   every-day non-stars, for a few
minutes in time, experience the
   butterflies, the challenge—the
pre-stage sweating palms:

Then it's
   lights, camera, action, through
the fantastic, talented, energetic director
   who molds the 'stars'. All the above
results in a greater understanding and
   respect for each of the technicians,
employees and guides, as well as
   the patient, polite, yet silent
costumed characters that
   roam the complex of
      Disney. I thank you.

"Ecstasy"

Love is magic when I see you
   exciting when we embrace
      tingling when you touch me
         ecstasy face to face.

My heart beats faster
   my senses reel in song
      you encompass my world
         and we respond as one.

"Erica, A Second Birthday"

Remember when you walked
  barefoot in the dewy grass
    holding onto Grandmas hand?

Was it only yesterday when
  I, walked with my grandma
    hand-in-hand, so long ago
      or was it just in fantasy land.

No. The memory is clear -
  withstanding years between,
    perhaps…someday, you too
      will hold another child's hand,

and remember…another
  sunny barefoot day,
    and share the mixed feelings
      of a moment, relived…
        from the past.

"Fractured Time of the Caregiver"

Decisions lead to distraction—disorder—delays.

Notes challenge—to expand—write.

Lists requiring attention - are unending.

An article that whispers, "what if?"—maybe later.

Headlines beam heartache, pride—why?—why not?

A job unfinished singes one's peace of mind,
   but filing it under later may turn into never –
     and left for someone else to ponder.

Interruptions—patience—life on pause.

Tear-stained reflection is OK. It comes framed and
   wrapped in a cloak of deception—then acceptance,
     but not buried—just an unplanned, unexpected journey,
       mixed with joy, love, frustration and support.

Friends suggested, "don't take it to heart"—but
   the thorns do sting—piercing—heart-shattering.

Smile! Work on mending and letting go,
   though like the stink of the skunk—it weighs heavy—
but dissipates with distance, prayer,
   and more prayer, and time.

However, determination, and moving forward—
   are the only acceptable answers.

Treasure the moments,
   and believe there are reasons
      for the detours.

"Honeysuckle Wine"

Masquerading as
   dancing goblets
in glossy white
   and sunshine gold.

The ghost-like
   delicate partners
ascend the
    continuous vine.

Enticing the
   hummingbird and
memories of
   hot summer's youth.

"Grandmas"

Grandmas are for loving
   and holding you close to their heart
when no one understands you
   and your world is falling apart.

Grandmas time is all consuming
   sharing your every care,
she understands and accepts you—
   expecting nothing, but is carefully aware

this binding friendship
   lasts beyond her lifetime, for
her timeless love lives within and
   is passed down generation,
     after generation.

"Haikus"

Warm spring winds orchestrated
    The Daffodil Waltz
Spattered by half-penny clouds

Spring Romance Abounds
   Geese attentively marching
     Pond gliding in pairs.

Gathered in an open field
    Buzzards puffin dance
For clusters of judging hens.

Spring winds orchestrate
The graceful Daffodil Waltz
    Blossom Baptism

"Home After Surgery

Don't expect to move like a dynamo dancer
  but more like a wounded bird.
Don't expect to be free of pain
  for it grabs at you like an avenging tigress.
  And unexpected naps are the norm.

No slenderizing, clinging trousers or skirts,
  try robes, caftans, loose fitting shirts.
To pick up a tea cup—equal to lifting weights.
  Don't even consider lifting a gallon of milk,
    stir-up a batch of cookies or bake a cake.

Imagine practicing being the gentle sergeant
  by polishing your pleeze and thank-yous.
Help—Help—Help—Help —Help—Help
  To sweep my floors, scrub the sink, fix
    the meals, write a letter, or reach a book.

For now my muscles have turned to gel
  and sag on my bony frame.
Excitement grew when I first washed my hair.
  Just bathing and dressing is a marathon,
    and a ride in the car, a tiring treat.

But I am thankful for loving hands
  and friends who care, a soft
round pillow to ease the aches.
  Six weeks have passed, and
    I can hardly wait—to lift the little
ones, drive the car, or use the stairs.

Of course, I'm thankful to be alive,
   and for the retention of
a female mirror image,
   yet a huge corner of my heart
still mourns the loss of

the hormone factory which
   triggered skin moisture,
elasticity, softness, muscle tone,
   strength, body scent, desire.
     But, Lord, will I ever get any
        any of it back?

"In Answer to a Prayer"

Do spirits really travel
   back and forth in time?

I question…
   because today, I felt at one with
a collage of ancestors and God,
   when sunset's eternal palette
slithered fiery red into blush
   of pink, cream, powder blue.

Then sunrise caught me—
   unaware. In awe—I stared.
I dared—to stop and breathe—in
   the spectacular freshness of dawn.

Embarrassed, that I had slipped.
   Forgot to thank you, God
for another perfect day. A bit of
   sunshine—a little rain.

But I've been busy, you know—searching,
   working towards that Goal—for that
someday that would be loaded with the
   fulfillment of all my expectations!

Then moonlight bowed to twilight.
   Sun burst the distant cloud, and my
loving dreams lay scattered on the lawn
   midst sparkling cathedral-type frosty
prisms, and a seldom-used open door.

While I had hoped for heaven tomorrow,
    patience plus determination revealed
my dreams were already here.
    Waiting. Here in my soul.

"It's About Time…"

While re-organizing my sewing/
craft room—discoveries took me
  down memory lane.

The IRS suggests saving seven years
  of the what, when, where and how
tax-payers spend their income. Thus
  our records were dutifully stashed
and forgotten.

Sifting through cancelled checks and
  twenty-five year-old itemized receipts
can be compared to reading through
  journals, or—the wonder of re-reading a
favorite book.

Looking back, when we were in the midst
  of the action, the happening, the
picturesque—we were just too absorbed to
  appreciate the joy and togetherness.

So. Marking the end of another year is
  like a birthday. The beginning of a
promising new year.

 It's time to start fresh. Dust the memories
  until they shine—sparkle—settle.
Resulting in unexpected fulfillment, with
  space and time to fill, feel, and explore.

"Let Me Tell You a Story"

Let me tell you a story…
   about a China Doll. She is 11" tall,
with eyes of blue, bow-shaped cherry-red
   lips, and rosy cheeks that brighten her
alabaster face. Deep waves of black hair
   frames her delicate ears. Two C-shaped curls
spill onto her fore-head. Her hands are curved
in a friendly manner, and her sawdust-filled body
   is firm, in black high-heeled China boots.

   She was all the rage in her time. Designed in
Germany in circa 1850, and cherished by the sister
   of Great, Great Uncle William Arza Llewellyn's wife,
Flora Belle's 70-year old sister who initiated the
   tradition in 1918, of passing-on this China Doll to
the eldest daughter when she turned Sixteen.

   Her fitted dress was peach silk, with matching
pantaloons trimmed in ecru lace and wrapped in folds
   of the same fabric. At birth, Edna, the first owner,
moved from Home in Continental, to Bradner, Fostoria,
   Green Springs, Norwalk, Old Fort, Lima and places in
between. When Marilyn turned sixteen, the China Doll's
   next home became a size five shoe box, on her
numbered shelf, space #402, inside the built-in oak
   cupboard in the Study, of the Girl's Cottage, at the
E.U.B. Flat Rock Children's Home in Flat Rock, Ohio.
   Valerie is her new owner.

The China Doll's sawdust body remains firm and
and warm—her face, hands and black boots,
   cool to the touch, a rarely-held fragile treasure.
Yet regardless of residence, she is still passed on
   to the daughter in line. Her features have not
faded. Although, she has an additional layer of
   fabric to protect her body, and her new dress
and pantaloons are a lovely green, and offers
   a family connection to be cherished.

"Mended?"

Life is precious.
   Time slips away
with the tenacity of
   a neglected toothache.

If your travel to and
   from work, before
and after daylight,
   and this politically

misunderstood Covid 19
   has separated family
and friends, try to restore
   this slippery, broken,

connection. It's like
   capturing a sunrise,
a sunset, a
     hovering fog.

But when voices lift
   in a gathering of the
Lord's energetic, haunting,
   harmony in song,

it reveals the joy of the
   Holy Spirit, possibly
mending this distance, with
   patience, acceptance, and time.

"My Shadow And Me"

Me and my
  shadow stand
outside the
  crowd alone.

Shadows
  appear on
sunny days and
  moonlit nights.

An illusion with
  no life, no future—
not my shadow
  without me.

Yet, without a
  compassionate
soul, there is
  no light within.

Anymore,
  only the Lord
knows my
  heart—my spirit—

  this underlying
    passion to
write, share,
inspire, love.
So shake the
  shadows. Live
life and soar.

"My Two Grandmas"

Grandma's best clothes smelled
  of moth balls, always neat as a pin,
plus a wrap-around apron with pockets.

Her kitchen smelled of soap and the
  burning wood cook-stove, fried
chicken, home made bread.

Breakfast was oatmeal topped with
  Wheaties, toast, Postum for them,
Ovaltine for me.

Both had Their rocking chair, too high
  for me, but one allowed me to sit on
her nice soft lap, the other did not.

One always had time for a hug, the
  other loved me too, in her own way.

One lived in the country. The other
  lived in town. With lessons learned
with God and nature.

And pretty is as pretty does 'oft rings
  within my heart, for she could read
between the lines—to the dismay of many.

It appeared they both walked away from
  us, my sisters and me, after we were
sent to the children's home. One glorified

our residence as a private school. I felt
   Dad's visits were doing his duty, however we could count on Mom's visits that were from love and missing us.

"New Beginnings"

She stepped into a gently rocking boat
   tied at the dock. Her footing was unsteady.
Fear left a sour taste. But, Lord, I can't
   swim! Water sloshed against the dock.

She could do this. She hugged her life-vest
   tight against her chest. Then, tugged the
rope loose from the brass ring—
   disconnecting her from the safety of
yesterday.

Digging her nails into the bench, she
   plopped down. The anchor lay at her
feet. The boat had two oars, plus a
   motor at her back.

She waited as the morning sun lit-up the
   horizon. The air was still. The boat didn't
move. She carefully tried one oar, but merely
   went in a circle. Some launching!

Gripping the compass, she prayed for
   guidance. Nothing happened. The sound of a
boat motor off in the distance was followed by
   a soft hum as they tied-up at the dock nearby.

She released the lanyard-held compass, set
   the oars aside, and announced, "I am headed
towards a new tomorrow. Anyone like to join me?"

She started the motor, and several boats followed her.

Why had it taken her so long to completely Trust in the Lord? And surprisingly, in the process—Believe in herself?

Ohio's October Masquerade

Mother Nature swirls
   her extravagant palette
in a haze of sunburst gold.

Miles of maple, dogwood,
   ash and oak trees
vie for attention yet harmonize,
   cloaked in October's masquerade.

From hillsides to manicured lawns,
   Jack Frost conspires to
paint leaf-bearing trees in
   momentary blends and splashes of
lemon, orange, peach, apple,
   butterscotch, cherry, rose,
strawberry, raspberry, lime,
   walnut and pecan.

Then, in a whisper of silence,
   the morning sun glints off a
shower of leaf-filled dew drops,
   mini-jeweled opal, topaz, ruby and pearl.

Attempting to fool us
   in the hesitation
between summer and winter,
   Ohio's October dyes,
shrinks, then sheds
   summer's dress, exposing

dormant, one-of-a-kind, naked,
   picturesque skeletons,
proudly resting, creaking, moaning,
   anticipating Spring.

"One Last Visit—One Last Goodbye"
Second Place in 2000 LAWC Poetry Contest

Rows of suckered tree stumps
   cast eerie, elongated morning shadows,
revealing spirits of a past once-thought
   long forgotten.

The crumbling weather-washed barn
   sways and leans against
the dependable golden willow guarding
   three moss-covered grave stones.

A rusted manure spreader,
   entwined in years of wandering
honeysuckle and wild grape
   is home to ground sparrows and rabbits.

The white bearded 'visitor' leans on his hand-hewn cane
   seeing instead…his wife, daughter and son picking
rows of apple and pear,
   a sound, straight-roofed barn
advertising Oh Henry! candy bars,
   a bright red manure spreader
drawn by his team, Dobbin and Bobbin.

Snow clouds move in shadowing the sun
   quickly blanketing the past in
picturesque white on white—preserving the
   like-new untarnished past for this his
last visit, his last goodbye.

"Our Annual Family Christmas"

For weeks, we clean, shop,
  bake the special holiday goodies,
rearrange the household and
  contemplate what to put where,
decorate the house—inside and out,
  shop and wrap each special gift
with loving care.

Family and guests finally arrive.
  The adults traipse in hugging covered
dishes, bags of gaily-wrapped gifts—
  as they corral the children questioning
how soon? The noise level escalates.

Bright lights and Christmas Carols have
  fore-shadowed and predicted the time is near,
like a wedding so tuned to the last minute rush.
  Paper soon clutters the crowded rooms while
oohs and ahhs, surprise, chuckles and laughter
  abound. Duty-bound for some, tradition for
others, but with unselfish love our family
  gathering spells Christmas.

Not forgetting six-handed euchre. One game
  that several generations continue to enjoy.
Teens look forward to when they can play.

Clusters of conversations, comradery, and mischief
 challenge time set aside for each other.
Afterwards, bits of paper, ribbon, and empty
 boxes lay scattered midst echoing laughter,
flashing colored lights, reflections of
 surprise and memories to store.

Then all too soon…treasures are gathered,
 warm hugs that pledge safe journey and loving
promises about next year's family Christmas.
 The house settles to calm. Christmas satisfaction
reflecting silent twinkling lights, warm memories
 of yet another crowded photo session.

"Our Thank You Love Anniversary Cake"
Published Dec. 1990 Senior's Beacon

Start with a measure of fate,
   timing—attraction.
Then add a pinch of instant action.

Blend in a scoop of trust,
   a touch of promise.

Texture with gentle respect,
   silent understanding.

Then bond with
   unquestioning love.

Toss in a handful of surprises,
   misunderstandings and
     communication gaps.

Flavor with humor.
   Bake with humble patience.

Frost with time.
   Decorate with interminable joy.

"Replaced"

The weather-stained porch
   had tumbled onto its
knees. The disconnected
   spouting wrapped in

the clutches of wild grape,
   honeysuckle, and wild rose;
dangled, creaked and twisted
   in the afternoon breeze.

Strands of dried perennials:
   lemon balm, lavender, and
mint, drifted from this summer's
   abandoned Robin's nest.

However, when they return in
   the spring, last year's nesting
place will have been replaced
   with concrete and steel.

So next year, they will have
   to move across the road
to the darkened woods, and
   start over in a new world.

"Research"

Looking for an
  ancestor connection,
a recipe, someone who
  moved or changed
    their phone number?

A word that makes
  your writing sing,
how to rewire a lamp,
  a car, a home,
a missing line or paragraph
  to finish a project?

Today's researcher
  depends on the internet.
Why waste time
  looking elsewhere?

But they miss the in-
  between connection—
the book that might or
  would have the answer,
or someone they know
  who would enjoy
    sharing.

"September into October"

September into October
  In Their Own Time

While Maple Trees accept the change
  of seasons, casting off their leaves of
    rust and gold,

Walnuts plunk by the basketsful—
  spring-green to mushy
    black and brown,

Tomatoes ripen in spurts—from
  green to yellow and red,

While Rhododendron is showy with a
  hint of wine—tiny blossoms of
lavender settle into beads of
  memorable historic fragrance.

Meanwhile, in a bed of May-blooming
  Irises, as they continue to gather
    strength for next spring,

one tall, proud Iris prepares to
  bloom a second time, before it
says its goodbye to September—
  greeting October with one more
lovely picture-perfect purple floral
  surprise, even though November

snow showers threatened—I
  enjoyed one bloom a week,
plus one more gutsy Bud
  impatient to bloom before
the killing frost, bloomed on
  a sunny Sunday morn.

"Snowy Sweet-Scene Dream"

Drift off with me into fall's snowy dreams,
   on picturesque clouds 'oer candy-land scenes.

Step lightly where frost-nipped caramel apples lay.
   and sidestep when icy strands of gold-willow taffy sway.

Where rain-blackened trees merge into licorice stick teams,
   marching through drifts of marshmallow crème.

Clutch bouquets of snowy chrysanthemum tops,
   quickened into baskets of frosted lemon drops.

Gather bunches of cattails from a muddy stream,
   dream-dipped chocolate bananas in peanut-butter cream.

Chase fall's painted leaves spritely fragile curls,
   wind tumbled, then rolled into orange nougat swirls.

Lick triple-dipped pistachio crème
   enticingly cone shaped like the evergreen.

Plod 'ore winter-plowed fields of brownie cakes'
   then skid swiftly home atop apple cider lakes

where sun reflected snowflakes gleam
   to wake me from my sweet-tooth dream.

"Slick—Sleet—Snow"

I opened the blinds of our
   bedroom window to the sight
of the beginnings of a snowman.
   There were three balls of snow.
But wait! How is that possible?
   There are no foot prints!

Releasing, pressuring, chasing
   the warm air east,
the wind howled and roared
   around our home all night;
dropping the temps to
   minus or below—and dumping
hail, sleet and slick—on the snow.

But before the morning calm,
   and with no snow to blow—
the wind used our backyard
   as a bowling alley.

Scooping, skipping into the
   snow's dimpled crust, these
frustrated surface winds
   left a trail of dips and skids;
resulting in Ohio's First
   Phenomenal "Snow Rollers."

Fields came alive as the wind
   played dodge-ball—rolling layers
of snow into pumpkin-sized
   boulders to weak baseballs.

The Lord does nothing half-way.
   Behold! Nature at its best.
What's next? Look out for an
   Oklahoma Panhandle Hook
     headed our way.

"Polar Vortex"

January 2014, an Arctic Polar Vortex swooped
   down into a weather jet-stream
   that screamed across the U.S.A.

Around Sunday noon, huge nickle-sized snow-flakes
   were dumped from clouds too tired to
   contain them, as they fell silently,
   urgently, threatening one's peace of mind.

Packing forty-five mile per hour winds—
   joined by bone chilling minus-zero temps, were
   then followed by sleet, rain, and more snow
   in the form of powdered sugar,
   resulting in dangerous white-out spaces.

Howling, demanding—the wind captured the snow
   like an artist's brush captures paint,
   poofing it into swirl-destined drifts—around
   anything in its path. An engineering feat, no doubt
   sweeping it into yards-long steps of scallops,
   shadowed indentations, landscaping icy crests—
   curving waves, peaks and valleys.

Come sun-up, the evergreens laden with ice
   and snow, bend towards the ground like
   lumbering giants brought to their knees,
   could barely sway—playing hide and seek,
   from the north, west and south-west winds.

The sky is blue. The sun casts shadows of a delicate sparkling ice encrusted apple tree.
But what is missing? No footprints? No wildlife anywhere? Except one crazy restless bird's attempt to fly—only to be flown backwards, should have been a warning.

"Spring & March Fog"

I was in my backyard and
called to my neighbor who was
 disappearing in a fog.

 Three little neighbor girls were
playing under a cluster of Blue
 Spruce didn't hear me either.

 Then, I glanced to my left and
a patch of fog was coming
 towards me. I rushed back to

 safety inside my house and woke
up. Imagine my surprise when
 moments later, I looked out my

 kitchen window, and my
backyard was a sea of fog. Was this
 morning's dream from the Lord?

 I am house-bound, due to the
eerie corona virus 19, the invisible
 enemy of mankind on this Planet.

 But, the Daffodils are in full bloom.
The Robins and Cardinals are already
 building nests, unaware.

"Stars To Hitch A Ride On"

Slow down world…
   Stop. Someone special
just left an empty space
   in our lives.

She filled our hearts
   with her bubbly
gift of gab,
   her love of music,
her honest welcome
   put all at ease.

She listened. And
   was there, when
her loved ones
   needed her.
They in turn—
   were there for her.

She left footsteps
   To follow.
Clouds to pin
   dreams on.
     Stars to hitch
     a ride on.

"Tasha, the Orphaned Lamb"

Tasha was born in the Spring, the first-born, of triplets on Howard Robinson's Suffolk Sheep Farm. Her sisters had white wool like their mom. But because Tasha was black, her mom butted her away. All the other lambs turned away as well.

Tasha was lost, and cried, Baa! Baa! Baa! She was hungry too. But Howard did not have the time to bottle-feed, even one of his herd of one-hundred. Tasha needed a new home where she would be loved and cared for.

Maddie was excited to see her Uncle Howard; but even more excited when she saw the little Black Lamb with a Happy Birthday Maddie bow around Tasha's neck. Family had prepared a bed-of-straw in a spacious stall for Tasha in Grandma Robinson's nearly empty barn.

Uncle Howard showed Maddie how to hold the special bottle of warm formula for Tasha. When Tasha tasted what was in the bottle, she tugged and gulped the formula, until the bottle was empty. Tasha was tired. She curled up against Maddie and fell asleep.

Tasha was also spoiled, and she practiced her instinctive butting skills whenever she could get away with it. However Maddie planned to show her at the county fair in the fall, which meant Tasha had to be halter-trained. Being different, and strutting like she was a Princess, won her the Grand Prize!

"The ABCs of My Roman Rooms"

Sleep even evaded meditation
   while a brilliant full moon
slipped slivers of light through
   my venetian blinds.

My mind drifted to the mental-
   placement of items round my
Roman Rooms. At the door of the
   Guest room, observe **Alpha**—

always first, then—Left to Right: **Bravo**—
   in a mirror, **Charlie**—a teddy bear
corner, **Delta**—a west window, **Echo**—
   a robin on a bench, **Foxtrot**—a round
picture, **Golf**—a travel bag, **Hotel**—the
   closet, **India**—white iron bed, **Juliet**—
swinging from the ceiling light.

To the master bedroom, observe **Kilo**—
   a stack of notebooks, then Left to
Right: **Lima**—vanity, **Mike**—on the radio,
   November—wall flowers, **Oscar**—
Souvenir bowling pin, **Papa**—pipe from
   Paris, **Quebec**—embroidered Canadian
Geese, **Romeo**—his closet, **Sierra**—quilt
   and **Tango**—ceiling shadows.

To the Sewing Room: **Uniform**—golf fairways in tapestry, **Victor**—Disney Shopping Bags, **Whiskey**—gift boxed in pine, **X-Ray**—box of negatives, **Yankee**—Christmas candle, **Zulu**—African Doll.

"Cocoon"

In a vacuum
   unaware of the surroundings
untouched by its hibernation.

Feeling no pain, no fear,
   no compassion, no love,
likened to the dead, among the living.

In a fog of self-deception,
   no warmth or cold
no sunshine or rain.

Detached.
   Sealed in the silent world of
the mind—in trauma,

 Pray God brings the springtime,
   releasing the butterfly
and heals the mind,
   an enlightened soul.

"Tri-Storied Barn"

Rows of suckered tree stumps
  beckon a wooded cemetery
    to life

alongside a five windowed,
  siding stripped, half
    naked barn.

Revealing aged timbers clutching to
  toothless, cathedral arched
    slatted windows.

Careless winds sigh
  through the
    empty cavern.

It's sagging roof leans
  wearily like an old man
    needing a cane.

Winter-dried vines tenaciously
  cling to rusted farm machinery,
    a sentinel of the past.

Tall pines offer morning
  shade ore' the moss
    covered overhang.

A towering willow
  draped in elegant gold
    whispers

to the crippled windmill of a time
   when life here was harsher,
      simpler, slower

now passed by, forgotten,
   fighting to retain
      its dignity.

"The Traveling Knight"
HM Ohio Poetry Day Association 2009
First Place 2001 LAWC Poetry Contest
Outstanding Performance from Ohio House of
Representatives 2009 OPDA contests

Like a knight in steel-girded armor
   he charges through the darkness
headlights piercing the silence,
    following a ribbon of
reflector-lit paths and glowing
   twin-red embers of
     the dragon before him.

Guard rails warn of depths unseen.
   shadowed hillsides of sheared stone
jut like a jagged black fortress, towards
   a sky-hung three-quarter moon.
Silent silhouetted evergreens stand
   like midnight sentinels, staunch
     protection against the unknown.

It's four in the morning.
   The knight sips hot coffee,
honors a sudden speed limit drop; and
   slows round a curve directly past
a shielded state patrol. Then detours
   for relief at a twenty-four-hour,
engine-running off-the-route, pit-stop.

Amber lights subtly reveal the
   posted highway routes.
While anticipation breeds anxiety,
   perspiration intermittently drips
from the questing engineer.

Arriving at their planned destination,
   the knight sighs with pride and
expectation, then silences the cycling
   horsepower, as a bursting sunrise
welcomes the weary warriors…
   travelers of the night.

"Turn Of The Century"

Nomads of the U.S.A.
  sell their homes, and
load their family
  into a mobile home.

With satellite guidance,
  travel across the U.S.A.
    to where the jobs are,

and park next to others
  who also found temporary
    employment.

Keeping their family
  together, these turn of
the century nomads venture
  across the U.S.A.
in search of their
  American Dream.

"Why People Downsize"

People downsize when
   loss of a job or promotion
forces them to re-locate,
   similar to the historic
great depression. Both
meant starting over.

If the parents wish to be a part
   of their children, and grandchildren's lives—they follow.
   And if the parents move, for
whatever reason—the family
   follows.

Retirees downsize their homes,
   their friends, their lifestyle,
as though patterned assumptions
   were the norm—not always a
choice. Like stepping-stones in
   reverse.

And shed a lifetime of memorabilia,
   to start over—with less obligations,
move to warmer climates, travel
   the world, or simply turn off the
freeway and cruise down the
   boulevard.

"Willie Nelson Performs Free Concert"

People came barefoot, with bodies oiled, dressed
   in jeans, shorts, red kerchief head-bands,
sun visors, cowboy hats, and tee-shirts
   that relayed numerous descriptions.

Beer and Pepsi flowed.
   friends greeted old friends and made new.
Shared stories, laughter and then surprise,
    when a hovering fog announced the
      ice cream vendor.

The country band tuned-up harmonica, and
   drums, plus electric acoustic, and bass guitars.
An attentive audience swayed and swooned,
   to "Blue Eyes Cryin' in the Rain." They danced,
and tapped their feet to the quickening beat
   leaving patterns in brown dust and grasses green.
They clapped their hands—in rhythm—to
   "Old Joe Clark"—forgetting the sweltering heat,
till intermittent breezes brought sighs of relief.

As the setting sun glared red from beyond the
   grandstand stage—blankets spaced like a
patchwork quilt were vacated, and gave way to
   a kaleidoscope of 35,000 standing fans as they
moved as a unit, to get closer to the stage.

They stretched on tiptoe for a snapshot or better
   view of Willie Nelson and Waylon Jennings as
they performed a free concert Friday, July 30 1982,
   at Ohio's Allen County Fairgrounds.

Then, while fans applauded—cheered—and
 whistled to "Under the Double Eagle"—
a Circling TV helicopter was politely ignored.

"You Needed A Makeover"

You needed a makeover…
   so you were transformed
from a mudroom/coat closet/
   pantry into an up-from-
the-basement laundry.

The washer and dryer are
   the main attraction with
soft-crème walls, and
   elegant sea-shell beige
cushioned tile flooring.

You have become a bright,
   fragrant, brand new
entrance to my kitchen. But,
   now where do I store my boots,
broom, mop and potatoes?

"If Today Were My Last"
HM in 2000 LAWC Poetry Contest

If today were my last day on earth,
   what would I do, pray tell…?
I'd say I love you to those I hold dear,
   make a phone call or two, I suppose,

Take a walk in the sunshine, the rain,
   crunchy snow. Watch a sunrise,
a sunset, the moon when its full.
   Laugh, cry, remember…

great times in the past, bake
   some cookies, wash my hair,
share a bouquet of lilacs, lavender,
   sage, thyme, mint leaves for tea.

Write a sonnet, set to music,
   for my epitaph, and give great
thanks to God for…granting me the
   time to love and be loved.

Then pray…
I leave footsteps to follow.
   Clouds to pin dreams on.
      Stars to hitch a ride on.

Author's Note

My writing was limited to my time, school assignments, and letter writing to Mom. Years later I signed-up for creative writing classes to improve my writing skills for the family histories.

I wanted to put together something special for a sister-in-law for her upcoming Fiftieth Wedding Anniversary party. I started by asking her questions about where the two of them had met. Her response was immediate.

"My sisters and I went to Lima's Schoonover Dance Hall against our Dad's wishes. He was against dancing. Period. That's where I met Clifford."

"Did he live in the area?"

"No. He was from Genera."

My questions of where they were married, who stood up for them, some of the places they lived after they were married, and where they had worked. The family really enjoyed reading the story with answers to questions they hadn't considered asking.

I had found something that I really enjoyed, and continued researching the family which grew into an annual Christmas Newsletter.

Several of the people who attended Creative Writing Classes directed by Catherine Bauer, were encouraged to organize a writer's club. The Lima Area Writers Club was born in 1980. We held a couple of writer's workshops and sponsored an annual area poetry contest, which was broken down into three categories: Adult, High School, and Grade school. One year we had 1,000 entries.

I was in the Lima Public Library at the Reference Department one day, when Mrs. Leffler stopped me and ask, "How would you like to write and get paid for it?"

She was the Feature Writer of her own column of the weekly *Enterprise*, published by Bob McDowell. Later she called me and asked if I would write about the history of LaFayette.

I read over some of her previous articles and thoroughly enjoyed gathering information and photographs. There was a man in town who proceeded to be my guide about a time when there wasn't an empty store front on Main. He pointed out where the grocery was, the barber, music store, library, a man who made cigars for sale, funeral director, doctor's office and news-paper in 1903, a general store, and farm equipment building.

My LaFayette story led me to others and Mrs. Leffler resigned and Mr. McDowell hired me. Six months later, he approached me and asked, "What do you think about us putting together a monthly paper for seniors?"

I was astonished. "You're asking me?" Truthfully, I can't recall exactly what I said after that, but when he admitted that putting out a senior's paper had been a dream of his, who could say no to that? Thus, the *The Senior's Beacon for the 55 and Older* was born. I became feature writer from March 1990 – May 1997, when the last paper was printed.

I attended press conferences for St. Rita's Hospice presentations at the Civic Center, was expected to find my own articles with accompanying photos, and wrote and recorded a 23-second radio commercial on Radio WCIT-AM. The most exciting part about writing these articles, was how the people I interviewed felt when the story came out in print.

While I was writing monthly articles for *The Senior's Beacon for the 55 and Older*, I had been granted one year to finish the coffee table book, *A Pictorial History of Lima/Allen County Ohio*, published in 1993. I had also started on my first novel, *The Flutist and the Dancer*, which was published in 1999.

Acknowledgments

I would like to thank all those who helped me clarify moments in my memoir:

My great nephew, Dean Welch, who helped me with a few dates when his family moved.

My great nephew, Daniel Stark, who shared his knowledge about trapping which was a way to control varmints that stole chickens and grain from the farmer. The trapper set their traps and checked them daily. The skins were called pelts and used for linings in hats and gloves.

My great nephew, Gary Gossman knew which apple his sister-in-law had chosen was the King Apple—amongst forty-six apple trees such as Yellow Delicious, Snow Apple and McIntosh to name a few. He took care of his mom and dad's orchard for four years as a project in FFA, and added that his grandpa had planted some of these trees.

My cousin, Michael Cramer, remembered visiting the farm where my mom and dad lived with their daughters when I was in the second grade. I remembered the farm, but not the second grade.

Charles Bates, Curator of Transportation (Railroad Archives) at the Allen County Museum, Allen County, Ohio.

Pat Rodabaugh for editing the stories in my memoir. She refused to touch my poetry.

Marilyn (bottom right) with her family

About the Author

Marilyn R. Stark graduated from Northwestern School of Commerce in Lima, Ohio. She has spent most of her life, writing and updating the family history of immediate and extended families. She also continues to mail over one-hundred annual Christmas Newsletters for her husband's family history. For six years, Marilyn was a Feature Writer for *The Senior's Beacon* (now out of print). She also wrote and recorded a monthly radio commercial for same. Her previous novels include *The Flutist and The Dancer, The Pianist and the Locksmith, Broken Arrows/Broken Promises, Trails End Isle and Wings, Safe Passage in Masquerade*, and *The Four Aces*. Of her memoir, she says, "Even after the publication of six novels and two historical books, the challenge of my personal memoir was written with humble, uneasy, persistent courage."

www.ingramcontent.com/pod-product-compliance
Lightning Source LLC
Chambersburg PA
CBHW040305170426
43194CB00022B/2896

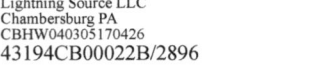